Do It!
ACTIVE LEARNING
in Youth Ministry

by Thom and Joani Schultz

Group
Books

Loveland, Colorado

Dedication

*To our son, Matthew, who sheds new light
and energy on active learning.*

Do It! Active Learning in Youth Ministry
Copyright © 1989 by Thom Schultz Publications, Inc.

Credits
Edited by Michael D. Warden
Book and Cover Design by Judy Atwood Bienick
Cover Photo by Joe Coca

Scripture quotations are from the Holy Bible, New International Version.
Copyright © 1973, 1978, 1984 International Bible Society. Used by permission
of Zondervan Bible Publishers.

ISBN 0-931529-94-8
15 14 13 12 11 10   03 02 01 00 99 98 97
Printed in the United States of America.

Contents

Introduction

Laughter, shouting and gentle teasing echoed off the canyon walls as eight young people and their youth leader hiked up the mountain trail. But nine teenagers had begun the hike earlier that morning.

No one noticed that Arnold had fallen behind.

In fact, people rarely noticed Arnold—ever. He was a quiet, pimple-faced kid. He started coming to Thom's youth group out of a desperate hope that someone would befriend him. But his shyness and lack of self-confidence seemed to make him invisible to the other kids.

At noon the mountain hikers stopped for lunch. Arnold finally caught up with the group and quietly sat on a boulder near Jennifer. She asked Arnold about his bulging backpack, which was stuffed with goodies. They talked for a half-hour before setting off for the summit.

This time Arnold didn't fall behind. In fact, he hiked at the front of the pack most of the way. His spirit seemed to soar. Somebody had actually noticed him.

When the group reached the mountaintop, Thom handed each person a 3×5 card with a small hole punched in the center. He asked the kids each to peer through the hole and discover something they hadn't noticed before. The kids spent a couple of minutes examining the mountaintop through their makeshift "cameras."

Then Thom asked the kids to tell what they discovered through their peepholes.

"That dead branch," said one.

"There's a bird's nest way up in the tree," another said.

"A rusted beer can," said another.

The last one to talk was Jennifer. She said, "I noticed that tiny blue wildflower over there."

Thom asked her how she felt about her discovery. "Well, it's such a beautiful little flower. And I almost stepped on it. I almost crushed this beautiful little thing. We all were in such a hurry to get to the top, we never noticed these tiny flowers."

"How is that like our group?" Thom asked.

Jennifer thought for a minute, then said, "It's exactly like our group." Some of the other kids giggled. "Arnold is that flower," she said. The giggles stopped. "Ever since Arnold joined our group, we've ignored him. I think we've walked right over him without ever noticing him—just like that flower. On the way up I got to talk with Arnold. I found out he's a neat person. I don't think we take enough time to stop and look—really look—for the good stuff in each other."

A soul-searching discussion followed. The young people made a discovery that changed their group from that point forward. They pledged to work together to uncover the God-given gifts in each other.

Using simple 3×5 cards, these young people experienced a change that altered their understanding of the world and their responsibility as part of God's family. They experienced active learning.

Through these pages we'll describe this process called active learning. You can master this fun process to guide your young people through powerful experiences that can enhance their spiritual growth.

You'll discover how your young people learn. You'll find out which methods (such as listening to sermons) often result in little learning. And you'll learn how to create fun experiences that actively involve all your kids and stimulate permanent understanding within them.

This book consists of two parts. Chapters 1 through 6 provide a foundation for active learning: guidance on how people learn, tips for creating your own active-learning experiences, and instruction on debriefing your learning activities. Chapter 7 contains a hefty collection of ready-to-use active-learning experiences.

We encourage you to embark on a new learning adventure through the concepts and practical programs found within these pages. And we'd love to hear from you as you explore active learning. Write to us:

Thom and Joani Schultz
Box 481
Loveland, CO 80539

CHAPTER 1

What Is Active Learning?

Active learning is, quite simply, learning by *doing*. It differs widely from the methodology we typically overuse in the church—passive learning.

Aircraft pilots know well the difference between passive and active learning. Their passive learning comes through listening to flight instructors and reading flight instruction books. Their active learning comes through actually flying the airplane or flight simulator. Books and classroom lectures are necessary, but pilots will tell you they really learned to fly by manipulating the plane's controls themselves.

Teaching young people how to live a Christian life is not unlike teaching young pilots to fly. Teenagers learn passively through reading the Bible, taking part in classroom discussions and listening to teachers' lectures. However, they'll really learn to "fly" through actual and simulated experiences. And like all student pilots, they'll make mistakes along the way. That's where you come in—to assure their ultimate safety and help them learn from their experiences.

In youth ministry, active learning may come to life in something as simple as a foot-washing experience or as exotic as a wilderness adventure week. Active learning may spring from a real-life experience, such as a workcamp. Or it may stem from a created or simulated experience in a classroom.

Examples include simulation games, role plays and purpose-ful games (games designed to produce a specific effect).

These simulated experiences are still real but in a different realm. In a way, they're like dreams. During simulations, as in dreams, students may experience real feelings such as fear, acceptance or anger. And where such feelings exist, learning usually takes place.

Visitors to any church's youth ministry can quickly see whether the leaders prefer passive or active learning. In the passive-learning churches, young people sit still (more or less) while an adult leader talks. In the active-learning churches, the visitor may find kids learning about leadership by building towers made of uncooked spaghetti or celebrating forgiveness by tossing confetti into the air.

Many youth workers find active learning uncomfortable. Some believe it's gimmicky: "You don't need to sit under a blanket to understand the concept of hiding from God." Some find it too taxing on their creativity: "I can't imagine how to make this lesson active." Some believe that lectures are the purest form of communicating the gospel: "That's how I learned about God. If it's good enough for me, it's good enough for these kids." Some simply fear trying something new. But these insecurities needn't keep us from venturing into the world of active learning with our students. With a little help, anyone can do it.

Active learning can increase any youth ministry's effectiveness—large or small. The activities described in this book work with a handful of young people or with hundreds or thousands. Larger groups explore active learning by breaking into small groups of four to eight people—typically with one adult per small group.

Characteristics of active learning

We can more fully explain active learning by exploring seven characteristics:

1. Active learning is an adventure. You can't predict exactly what will happen once a person or group embarks on the journey. Active learning provides many surprises.

Not long ago we designed an active-learning experience to explore the issue of cliques in our youth group. We asked participants to form small groups and use newspapers and tape to build "walls" around themselves. Everyone joined in the experience except one girl. She crossed her arms and refused to participate with her assigned group. Later during debriefing, everyone shared discoveries. Finally the girl spoke up: "I need to apologize. I didn't participate because I thought this whole thing was uncool. I realize now that I built walls around myself by being too cool. And I separated myself from the rest of you. It just hit me that I probably do that all the time. Forgive me. I need to change."

We couldn't have predicted that outcome. But real learning took place.

Passive learning, however, is almost always predictable: Students sit passively while the teacher or speaker follows a planned outline or script. Students learn the intended specific lesson of the day—or so the teacher hopes.

In active learning, kids may learn lessons the teacher never envisioned. Because the leader trusts students to help create the learning experience, kids may venture into unforeseen discoveries. And often the teacher learns as much as the students.

When embarking on active-learning adventures, we must prepare ourselves to seize teachable moments—even if they surprise us. We must trust the Holy Spirit to touch our students in unexpected ways.

2. Active learning is fun and/or captivating. Among many young people, learning has gained a poor reputation. We often hear Christian educators and youth leaders say: "I get so frustrated with my kids. They're great at playing group games, but when the time comes to get serious and settle down for the lesson, they grumble and groan. All they want is fun."

That reminds us of the Sunday school teacher who yelled at her kids: "Shut up, you disrespectful incorrigibles! You'll never amount to anything! If you want to go to hell in a handbasket, then go right ahead! See if I care! Now, let's turn to our lesson on grace." She taught nothing but inconsistency. We do the same if we tell kids: "Okay, fun's over. It's time to learn."

Many people assume that fun and learning can't occur at the same time. But if young people find the lesson boring, they're probably not learning. Or if they are learning, their new knowledge probably won't stay with them long. Think back to your own teenage-student days in school or church. How many facts or important concepts do you remember from your teachers' lectures? Did you gain much knowledge?

The ability to absorb knowledge and insight comes from God, as does the ability to nourish our bodies. We eat well when the food tastes good and looks appealing. But many of us might starve if all food were tasteless and unappetizing.

Through lectures and sterile discussions we can force-feed our students a lesson on forgiveness. Or we can give them an opportunity to feast upon an active-learning experience by having kids burn sheets of paper on which they've listed their personal sins.

Active learning intrigues kids. When students find a foot-washing experience captivating or maybe a bit uncomfortable, they learn. And often they learn on a deeper level than any teacher's lecture could reach.

3. Active learning involves everyone. No passive spectators exist in active learning. Here the difference between passive and active learning becomes clear. It's like the difference between watching a football game on television and actually playing in the game.

Yes, you can learn about a football game by watching it on television. But you'll learn far more and remember the game longer if you join the team and play.

The often-used "trust walk" provides a good example of active learning in youth ministry. Half the group dons blindfolds; the other young people serve as guides. The "blind" young people trust the guides to lead them through the building or outdoors. The guides prevent the blind kids from falling down stairs or tripping over rocks. Everyone needs to participate to learn the inherent lessons of trust, faith, doubt, fear, confidence and servanthood. Passive spectators to this experience would learn little. Participants learn much.

The key word is involvement. If everyone gets involved—actively involved—everyone learns.

4. Active learning is student-based, not teacher-based. Active learning depends on students making discoveries, rather than teachers imparting facts and ideas. Active learning starts with students and moves at their pace. It allows time for unplanned topics to emerge. Though kids may cover less teacher-chosen material, they may actually learn more because of the student-oriented process.

You can often discern a leader's teaching style (student-based or teacher-based) by the way the leader arranges the chairs in the classroom. In passive, teacher-based settings, the chairs typically face the podium where the teacher delivers lectures. In student-based settings, the leader may place the chairs in small circles, push them to the side or arrange them in a creative maze.

Active-learning teachers make discoveries right along with the students. These teachers fully participate in the journey, experiencing the unexpected joys and sorrows at every turn. Active-learning teachers act as safari guides on an unpredictable adventure—rather than as all-knowing professors who've already arrived.

5. Active learning is process-oriented. In passive learning, the teacher typically delivers the lesson and expects the students to retain it. But active learning involves students in discovering the lesson. *How* kids arrive at the answer is as important as the answer itself, because they discover the reasons behind the conclusions they draw.

For example, our young people can passively listen to us preach about serving the poor. Or we can involve them in a service project where they learn why it's important for Christians to serve "the least of these." They'll experience the joy of giving without expecting anything in return. They'll feel gratitude from those they serve. They'll discover they can make a difference in someone's life. They'll experience the selfless love Jesus wants them to show.

These insights rarely come from merely listening to a message. They form through the process of living the experience and then debriefing the experience with skilled leaders' help.

Rather than always telling kids what to do, process-oriented leaders help their students learn how to make Christ-centered decisions.

6. Active learning is focused through debriefing. Experiences that you don't follow up with debriefing may carry little long-term value. Without debriefing, the trust walk mentioned earlier may linger in young people's memories as merely an interesting exercise. To draw real Christian understanding from this experience, debriefing as a group is necessary.

Debriefing—or evaluating an experience by discussing it in pairs or small groups—helps focus the experience and articulate its meaning. Through debriefing, leaders make sure that the group's experiences don't drift along unquestioned, unrealized, unintegrated or unorganized. Debriefing helps sort and order the information students gather during an experience. It helps learners relate the just-experienced activity to their lives.

Debriefing surfaces the general principles operating in an action. Kids then can apply those principles to other circumstances that arise in their lives.

7. Active learning is relational. Because active learning involves everyone and because all experiences are debriefed with other people, students must interact with each other. Passive learning can be a solitary experience, but active learning happens in fellowship with others.

Active learning, particularly during debriefing, requires that students reveal a bit of themselves to others. This offers a rare opportunity for honing interpersonal skills in our fast-paced world.

Please notice our use of the word "relational." Many youth ministries use this term yet ignore active learning. When they say "relational" they refer only to the relationship between the adult leader and the kids. That approach is fine, but it abandons one of the most powerful influences in adolescent life: peers. "Relational" in active learning refers to all the relationships in a group: adult to kid, kid to kid, and adult to adult.

GROUP Magazine research shows that the main reason kids come to youth groups is friends. Active learning capitalizes on this relational need. It encourages young people to learn from each other.

When young people, along with adults, share an experience and together debrief what happened, real learning occurs.

CHAPTER 2

Learning in the Church

The church has traditionally placed much confidence in passive learning. We've educated our kids primarily with sermons and scripture-reading, ignoring more active learning methods. Congregational singing comes closer to active learning than anything else most churches do.

Observe how most church worship centers are designed: rows of long wooden benches, bolted to the floor, all facing the pulpit. The furniture beckons us to sit still and listen. We look at the back of the person sitting in front of us. The arrangement discourages interaction. The very architecture ensures passive learning's dominance.

However, passive learning methods have their place. We can't learn everything actively. Reading is passive, but it greatly strengthens our understanding of the world around us. The scriptures have survived for centuries and inspired millions. Jesus, even as a young boy, modeled the value of reading God's Word. (Besides, if we didn't believe in the written word, why should we expect you to read this book and gain anything from it?)

And oratory is a gift. Countless lives have changed after hearing the gospel presented orally. Leaders often use sermons and youth talks to effectively influence kids' lives.

Many leaders, however, overuse the spoken word in the

church. Many youth ministries still rely solely on "the talk" to do all the "important stuff": attract kids to church, convert them to Christianity and build them into committed disciples. These same youth ministries may use active games and crazy skits to capture attention. But they freely admit they use such activities merely as lures to bait the kids into listening to the speaker. The talk—and nothing but the talk—does the "real" ministry.

Did Jesus place all his hope in the talk? Let's see.

Jesus and active learning

For centuries now, the church has communicated the gospel through written and spoken words. But the Christian life involves more than talk. Take a look at God's definition of the Word found at the beginning of John's Gospel:

In the beginning was the Word, and the Word was with God, and the Word was God. He was with God in the beginning. The Word became flesh and made his dwelling among us (John 1:1-2, 14a).

You see, God views the Word as active—manifested through his Son's active life. The Word, embodied in Jesus Christ, never came across as passive.

Jesus, the master teacher, used many forms of communication and many forms of teaching. He immersed people in experiences of all kinds—healing some, feeding others and casting out demons in still others. He even manipulated the weather to teach his disciples a lesson (Matthew 8:23-27). He used everything around him to enhance his teaching: little children, dirt, water, wine, clothing, trees, grains of wheat, sheep, goats and a Roman coin.

And yes, Jesus also taught through the spoken word. He was, without doubt, a talented orator. However, his speaking focused on active commitment. Jesus didn't say, "Just sit here and listen to me." He said, "*Follow* me." Active words.

The Bible overflows with action language. In fact, Jesus

frequently used active learning's core theme: *"Do, then learn."* Consider these episodes:

● **The rich young man**—Jesus said, "If you want to be perfect, go, sell your possessions and give to the poor, and you will have treasure in heaven. Then come, follow me" (Matthew 19:21). *Do, then learn.*

● **Storm on the lake**—Jesus said, " 'You of little faith, why are you so afraid?' Then he got up and rebuked the winds and the waves, and it was completely calm. The men were amazed and asked, 'What kind of man is this? Even the winds and the waves obey him!' " (Matthew 8:26-27). *Action, followed by lesson. Do, then learn.*

● **Healing on the Sabbath**—Jesus said, " 'You hypocrites! Doesn't each of you on the Sabbath untie his ox or donkey from the stall and lead it out to give it water? Then should not this woman, a daughter of Abraham, whom Satan has kept bound for 18 long years, be set free on the Sabbath day from what bound her?' When he said this, all his opponents were humiliated, but the people were delighted with all the wonderful things he was doing" (Luke 13:15-17). *Action, followed by lesson. Do, then learn.*

● **The woman caught in adultery**—Jesus said, " 'If any one of you is without sin, let him be the first to throw a stone at her.' Again he stooped down and wrote on the ground. At this, those who heard began to go away one at a time, the older ones first, until only Jesus was left, with the woman still standing there. Jesus straightened up and asked her, 'Woman, where are they? Has no one condemned you?' 'No one, sir,' she said. 'Then neither do I condemn you,' Jesus declared. 'Go now and leave your life of sin' " (John 8:7b-11). *Action, followed by lesson. Do, then learn.*

● **Washing the disciples' feet**—Jesus said, " 'You do not realize now what I am doing, but later you will understand.' When he had finished washing their feet, he put on his clothes and returned to his place. 'Do you understand what I have done for you?' he asked them. 'You call me "Teacher" and "Lord," and rightly so, for that is what I am. Now that I, your Lord and Teacher, have washed your feet, you also should wash one another's feet' " (John 13:7, 12-14). *Action, followed by lesson. Do, then learn.*

Jesus' quote during the foot-washing could be a slogan for active learning, "You do not realize now what I am doing, but later you will understand." That's the essence! Big lessons come through life experiences. And often we don't even realize we're learning something profound. Reflecting on an experience focuses and cements its lesson in our hearts. After the foot-washing, Jesus asked, "Do you understand what I have done for you?"

Jesus understood the workings of the human mind. He knew the disciples would never grasp servanthood or God's nature until they experienced something dramatic. He could have just explained the concept, but he wanted to deliver a knockout punch they'd never forget.

So God's Son dropped to his knees and gently cleansed his followers' filthy feet. Peter exploded, "No, you shall never wash my feet." But Jesus persisted. And Peter learned— through experience.

Yes, Jesus used storytelling and other more passive forms of teaching. But he creatively interspersed these with active-learning episodes—thereby strengthening and galvanizing a message that will live forever.

The active Word of God

The Bible, from cover to cover, details God's use of active learning. Abraham actively demonstrated the depth of his faith by raising his knife over Isaac (Genesis 22:1-13). Jonah learned about his inability to hide from God only after spending a little time in a fish's belly (Jonah 2:1-10).

God could have limited his teaching approach to the Ten Commandments (Deuteronomy 5:7-21), left for all to read. But that would have generated only limited educational results. So God proved (and continues to prove) his love and concern through action after action in his people's lives.

God uses a variety of methods to transform our hearts. He's not limited to passive-learning approaches. He believes in *"Do, then learn."* Can we? Can we break away from our less effective forms of Christian education? Can we take a hint from God himself about how we might better educate our people? The Bible records the story of God's people learning through experience. Are we modern mortals somehow different? Will passive, more academic forms of education do the whole job of communicating the gospel to our people today?

Dr. F. Earle Fox writes:

> . . . without exception all of the successful reform movements in the church have been non-academic (not anti-academic) but rather experiential in nature—from the early desert fathers, through the Benedictines, the Franciscans, the Jesuits, the Quakers, Methodists, right down to the present day "charismatic renewal." All this was not to the exclusion of serious academic work. But it was the experience that came first which provided the fodder for the rational mind to work upon. The Judeo-Christian tradition is profoundly experiential, not to the exclusion of reason, but as the precondition of it. That is, the material upon which reason exerts itself is precisely those experiences of ours which need ordering and coherence.[1]

Do, then learn. In active learning, we act our way into a new way of thinking, rather than think our way into a new way of acting.

Endnotes

[1] F. Earle Fox, "The Spiritual Core of Experiential Education," in *The Theory of Experiential Education* (Boulder, CO: Association for Experiential Education, 1983), 100.

CHAPTER 3

How We Learn

Think about yourself for a moment. Think back to a big lesson you learned in life. Close your eyes and concentrate.

Now identify how you learned that lesson:

● Did you learn your big lesson by reading about it somewhere?

● Did you learn it by listening to someone's speech or sermon?

● Or did you learn it from an experience you had?

Most of us learn our big lessons in life through our experiences. What happens to us colors how we view the world. To a large extent, our lives are shaped not by what we hear in speeches or read in books, but by what we experience.

Our active learning began when we were tiny babies. University of Chicago sociology professor James S. Coleman writes:

> For a child who has seen a grandparent grow old and die, the words "old age" and "death," have a rich fabric of meaning unknown to the child without such experience. And when the child grows up, and reads news stories about nursing homes and participates in political decisions about the elderly, the fabric of meaning provided by those experiences provides a context for action that is otherwise missing.[1]

To better understand how we learn, let's look at the two primary learning processes: passive and active. In youth ministry and Christian education we use both. Knowing how each method works can help us design the most effective mix.

First, let's examine passive learning. Some call passive learning the "banking" concept of education—information is simply deposited in storage receptacles.

Passive-Learning Process

1. Information is received. Information reaches the students through a symbolic, coded medium: words, books, lectures, sermons. Students remember the information.

2. Information is organized. Students observe and understand a general, biblical principle.

3. Specific applications are derived from the biblical principle. Students perceive ways to apply the principle to their lives.

4. Knowledge is applied. Students act on what they've learned.

As an example, let's see how the passive-learning model teaches young people about the harmfulness of cliques. The passive teacher might ask kids to sit and listen to a talk on the subject. The students hear the speaker's words and understand the main principle: As Christians we should never exclude people. The teacher then guides the young people to see how this principle applies to their behavior when new kids join the youth group. When the students come back next week they warmly include the newcomers.

That's how it works when students with good cognitive abilities use passive learning.

Now let's look at active learning. You'll see that this process works in almost a reverse sequence from the passive model.

Active-Learning Process

1. Action is undertaken. Students share an experience in a particular situation.

2. Particular effects are understood. Students learn consequences from the situation.

3. A general principle is understood. Through active discussion, students discover the biblical principle at work in this situation.

4. The principle is applied. Students put their knowledge into action in a new circumstance.

Now let's see how our clique lesson might change by using the active process. The leader asks kids to form groups of five or six, then instructs the person wearing the most white in each group to step away from the group. The teacher then asks each group to lock arms and keep the white-clad member from penetrating the circle. The white-clad kids try to force their way into their circles using whatever methods they choose.

After the kids struggle, tickle and laugh for a while, the leader asks the groups to discuss the experience. Some young people discover they experienced a certain glee in keeping the white-clad ones out. Others feel guilt. And the white-clad kids say they experienced rejection and felt like giving up. Some kids suggest this simulation reminds them of cliques in the youth group. After further discussion, the students understand the general principle: As Christians we should never exclude people. At the next meeting the students warmly include newcomers.

That's how growth occurs when leaders employ the active-learning process.

Various learning methods

Which of the two processes—passive or active—results in the most long-term gain? Edgar Dale, former professor of education at Ohio State University, conducted a classic study of the effectiveness of various teaching tools. He ranked these 10 methods in the form of a cone, with the most effective appearing at the base. (See diagram on page 27.)

"The Cone of Experience" depicts a variety of learning approaches, all of which can prove successful in youth ministry. Each can be enhanced by supplementing the teaching with other methods on the scale.

The top of the cone shows learning methods that rely on other people's experiences. These methods require little student involvement and result in relatively little learning.

The bottom shows methods that require the learner to experience certain situations. "Direct, purposeful, personal experiences" depend on the full involvement of the learner—senses, mind and body. Such experiences might include creating an idea (such as wanting to build a tree house); designing a plan (drawing a blueprint for the tree house); using resources (purchasing and working with the needed lumber and tools); and taking responsibility for an outcome (testing the tree house's sturdiness by climbing into it). This level of involvement results in maximum learning.

"Contrived experiences" provide almost as much learning potential as direct, purposeful personal experiences. These contrived activities can be performed in the classroom. Games, simulations and role plays, when carefully planned and later debriefed, can result in real learning with lasting implications.

Studies reveal that the more students become involved in an experience, the more they'll learn from it. The chart on page 28 shows average retention rates of different learning methods.

It's sobering to admit that our most-used learning methods in the church produce the least results. Stubbornly we hope our students will memorize and retain all we tell them and assign them to read.

Testing our own levels of retention from our student days may help us accept the truth. For example, how much memorized information do we remember from our junior

The Cone of Experience

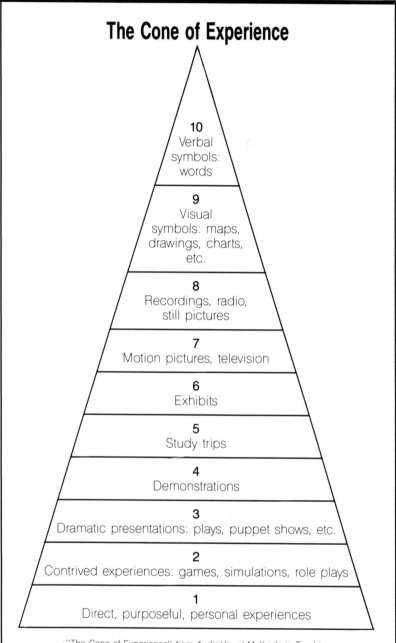

10
Verbal
symbols:
words

9
Visual
symbols: maps,
drawings, charts,
etc.

8
Recordings, radio,
still pictures

7
Motion pictures, television

6
Exhibits

5
Study trips

4
Demonstrations

3
Dramatic presentations: plays, puppet shows, etc.

2
Contrived experiences: games, simulations, role plays

1
Direct, purposeful, personal experiences

Average Retention[2]

Spoken or written communication	Media	Role play	Direct experience
5-10%	25%	40-60%	80-90%

high school history classes? Or how many sermons, youth talks or traditional Bible studies we attended as teenagers can we now recall?

So why do we continue to pour messages into our kids' heads solely through lectures or discussions? Well, as leaders we know our information is important. It's meaningful to us. And we have so much to say and so little time to share with our young people. Too often we desire to control all the information entering our kids' heads. Perhaps our own egos sweep us into believing that our special communication prowess will beat the odds, that our words will magically stun our kids into retaining everything we say.

But they won't.

A couple of years ago Bob and Valerie, youth leaders at a local church, planned a weekend retreat for their high school group. They paid a well-known speaker $400 to deliver several talks during the weekend. The speaker kept the kids spellbound. If anybody could touch these kids, he could.

Recently Bob and Valerie asked their kids to recall the highlights from that weekend. No one mentioned the speaker.

A couple of kids mentioned the water fight between the guys and girls. But most remembered the real highlight: the caper of the missing purse. Debbie awoke in her cabin one morning and couldn't find her purse. Everybody suspected Joe, a new kid who was a loner. Joe denied taking the purse, but the guys sneaked into his cabin and ransacked his stuff looking for it. Later Debbie found her purse in the shower room, right where she had left it. Bob and Valerie called the young people together to talk about their actions. After a few feeble excuses they all apologized to Joe, gave him a group hug and prayed for forgiveness.

Those kids learned a lot from that retreat. But nobody can recall who the speaker was or what he talked about.

While passive-learning methods such as lectures have their place in youth ministry, too often we overestimate their long-term effectiveness. Passive methods work best when combined with active methods—to help focus and maximize the message. Jesus used this one-two approach extensively: a dramatic action combined with a short talk or discussion.

When we involve our students in direct experiences, they'll remember and understand. The old adage "Use a word three times and it's yours" gives us a clue about affecting our students' behavior. The adage doesn't urge us to *hear* a word three times or *read* a word three times, but to *use* it three times. Only then will we permanently add the word to our vocabulary. Usage is action. And action becomes a part of our personal history.

The words of a poster clarify with wonderful simplicity the value of active learning:

> Tell me, and I'll forget.
> Show me, and I may remember.
> Involve me, and I'll understand.

Teaching a new generation of learners

The need for active learning in youth ministry is greater today than in generations past. Today's media-wise teenagers get bored easily. They've grown up in an unprecedented kaleidoscope of media images, concert extravaganzas, video games, computer wizardry, and a high-tech explosion of information. Our longstanding approaches to Christian education don't stand a chance in our teenagers' fast-paced world.

John I. Goodlad, in his book *A Place Called School*, writes: "For most students academic learning is too abstract. They need to see, touch and smell what they read and write about. Time spent visiting a newspaper press, examining artifacts or observing a craftsman provides reality and stimulus for later reading, explaining and discussing."[3]

In youth ministry, active forms of education are growing while passive forms are losing their luster. Parachurch youth organizations such as Young Life and Youth for Christ no longer attract the large crowds of young people they did in their heyday. Their club meetings anchored by passive lectures worked better in the '60s and '70s than they do today.[4]

Church-based youth ministries using active learning have grown—both in numbers and effectiveness. Young people respond well to involvement-style classroom learning, such as the active experiences described in this book. In addition, many churches now involve their teenagers in direct, purposeful experiences called workcamps or mission trips. GROUP Magazine's workcamp program grows every year and now attracts thousands of young people every summer. Kids come with their youth groups to weeklong camps of volunteer service. They work in small teams repairing needy families' homes.

Once a young person experiences a workcamp, he or she typically returns year after year. Why? Often the workcamp provides young people the first opportunity to put their faith into action. The gospel finally makes sense. They see, firsthand, the effects of "love your neighbor." They realize they can make a difference in the world. One 16-year-old girl said: "If we wouldn't have come here, this lady's roof never would've gotten fixed. Because of me she'll be warm this winter. That really gives me a good feeling." Workcamps build self-esteem.

And workcamps build relationships. Young people work together to accomplish a common goal. They're compelled to interrelate, to make friends, to polish interpersonal skills. Such interaction fills a real need in our impersonal age of computers, television, videos and Walkmans. Today's kids crave people-to-people experiences. And workcamps provide a concentrated dose of it—with peers, adult leaders and the residents kids serve.

Workcamps work with Christian young people because they're solid examples of active learning. We could choose to lecture kids about servanthood. We could give them reading assignments. But only real experiences deliver this kind of life-transforming power.

Endnotes

[1]James S. Coleman, "Experiential Learning and Information Assimilation: Toward an Appropriate Mix," *The Theory of Experiential Education* (Boulder, CO: Association for Experiential Education, 1983), 131.

[2]Jim Burns, *The Youth Builder* (Eugene, OR: Harvest House Publishers, 1988), 184.

[3]John I. Goodlad, *A Place Called School* (New York: McGraw-Hill Book Company, 1984), 128.

[4]Thom Schultz, "What's Happened to Young Life and Campus Life," GROUP Magazine (May 1985), 16-23.

CHAPTER 4

Our Sensory Preferences

W hen we jump into active learning, our students will use many of their senses. And we may discover that some kids learn better using certain ones. That's normal. We're all different.

To help you discover how *you* might learn best, how you typically experience the world, we've devised a little quiz. Take a moment to fill it out. It's fun!

Experiencing Your World

For each question, select one response that best matches your reaction to the question. Go quickly, without much deliberation; mark the response that initially strikes you as best.

1. How do you think of snow on an early winter morning?

_____a. a blanket of white everywhere

_____b. silence and peacefulness

_____c. cold and frosty

2. Imagine you're a scuba diver. What impresses you most about your first dive to 60 feet below the surface?

_____a. watching the fish swim by

_____b. hearing your breathing in the underwater silence

_____c. feeling weightless

3. When talking with a friend, how are you most likely to respond?

_____a. "I see what you mean."

_____b. "I hear what you're saying."

_____c. "I know how you feel."

4. Think of the house of your favorite grandparent (or some other beloved relative or person from your childhood). Do you ever encounter places that remind you of this house? What usually triggers these memories?

_____a. similar architecture, furniture or decorating

_____b. a familiar sound (such as a creaking floor, noisy fan or Lawrence Welk music)

_____c. a familiar smell (such as baking, mustiness or disinfectant)

5. Imagine you've been asked to give a speech to a large group of people you admire. You're nervous. How do you feel as you step to the podium?

_____a. "There are a thousand eyes out there looking at _me!_"

_____b. "What if they don't like what I'm going to say?"

_____c. "It feels like I've got a thousand butterflies in my stomach!"

6. What is most prominent in your memory about your visits to the dentist?

_____a. the hovering dentist thrusting his tools into your mouth

_____b. the sound of the drill

_____c. the pain

7. Imagine you've just attended a rousing Broadway musical. What did you like best?

_____a. the dancing, costumes, dazzling sets

_____b. the singing, the orchestra, the music

_____c. the exhilaration

8. The President is coming to your house to "get close to the people" and explain his policies. What would you most surely do?

_____a. have your picture taken with the President

_____b. listen carefully to what he has to say

_____c. shake the President's hand or give him a hug

9. Imagine someone has just made a presentation for starting a new program in your church. The presenter was an inspiring speaker and came prepared with handouts. You like the speaker's idea. What would you likely say?

_____a. "It looks good to me."

_____b. "It sounds good to me."

_____c. "I feel good about this idea."

10. Imagine you're present during Jesus' ministry 2,000 years ago. Which of the following would you most like to experience?

_____a. see him perform a miracle

_____b. hear him teach

_____c. feel him touch you or heal you

Count the number of "a" responses, "b" responses and "c" responses.

If you marked mostly "a" responses, you're probably visually oriented. You may tend to learn best and remember more by what you see. Looking at symbols that represent concepts may help you.

If most of your choices were "b" responses, you probably prefer auditory stimuli. Your ears may be your favorite information-receivers. Sounds seem to stick in your memory.

If you marked mostly "c" responses, you may be most "in touch" with your kinesthetic sense—touch. You may tend to remember more about what you touch or use with your hands. However, the "c" response in question four may also reveal sensitivity to the sense of smell.

Notice how certain sensory preferences are revealed in our use of vocabulary. Check your responses to questions three and nine. In fact, we can often determine people's preferred senses by listening to their language. If a person says "I see what you mean" a lot, he or she is likely visually oriented. And we may find teaching this person most successful when we use visual teaching methods. The chart on page 37 shows you how to listen for different people's preferred senses.

In addition to kinesthetic, visual and auditory preferences, some people lean toward the gustatory—sense of taste. Others prefer the olfactory—sense of smell.

This exploration into how different people interpret the world reminds us of the importance of varying our active-learning activities. Because everyone learns differently, our planned experiences should, over time, focus on as many senses as possible. Some examples:

● **Kinesthetic**—Students empathize with Christ by holding their arms outstretched for an extended time. (See page 107.)

● **Visual**—Students see the harm of hurling putdowns by "stoning" each other with foam-rubber rocks. (See page 60.)

● **Auditory**—Students study the parable of the vine-

How We Experience the World[1]

Meaning	Kinesthetic	Visual	Auditory
I (don't) understand you.	What you are saying feels (doesn't feel) right to me.	I see (don't see) what you are saying.	I hear (don't hear) you clearly.
I want to communi-cate some-thing to you.	I want you to be in touch with something.	I want to show you something (a picture of something).	I want you to listen carefully to what I say to you.
Describe more of your pres-ent expe-rience to me.	Put me in touch with what you are feeling at this point in time.	Show me a clear picture of what you see at this point in time.	Tell me in more detail what you are saying at this point in time.
I like my experience of you and me at this point in time.	This feels really good to me. I feel really good about what we are doing.	This looks really bright and clear to me.	This sounds really good to me.
Do you understand what I am saying?	Does what I am putting you in touch with feel right to you?	Do you see what I am showing you?	Does what I am saying to you sound right to you?

yard workers by vocally participating in the reading of an updated version of the story. (See page 127.)

● **Gustatory**—Students share in a "feeding of the multitudes" by dividing a small bit of bread among many people. (See page 85.)

● **Olfactory**—Students understand the humility of Jesus by experiencing the smells of his birthplace—holding a Bible study in a stable or bringing animal dung and hay to the classroom.

Endnotes

[1] John Grinder and Richard Bandler, *The Structure of Magic II* (Palo Alto, CA: Science and Behavior Books, Inc., 1976), 15.

CHAPTER 5

Creating and Leading an Active-Learning Experience

Your young people learn and grow from two different types of active-learning experiences: serendipitous and planned.

Serendipitous experiences happen unexpectedly. For instance, your church van breaks down on the way to the retreat, the electricity goes off during a lock-in, your annual carwash brings in $1,000 instead of the usual $200, or only three kids show up for your Giant New Year's Eve Blowout. These present real opportunities for learning. An alert leader will always be ready to say "Hey, let's talk about this" and begin the debriefing process.

The other type of active learning encompasses planned activities. However, planned experiences may produce a few unplanned twists and outcomes.

Planned experiences fall into two categories: direct, purposeful experiences and simulated or symbolic experiences.

Direct, purposeful experiences include service projects, workcamps, caroling, cooking as a group, camping, banner-making—any activity designed to produce a useful product or service beyond the active learning itself. Even though students usually don't realize they're learning anything, such experiences generate the highest potential for learning. They also usually require more planning and preparation.

It's difficult to provide direct, purposeful experiences in youth ministry on a weekly basis because of all the planning involved. For that reason, we frequently use the other type of planned activity—simulated or symbolic experiences. These can produce almost as much learning as direct experiences and can be staged at any time, in any place. They include simulation games, role plays, participatory drama, active case studies and art projects. To the uninformed, these types of learning experiences may resemble mere play, but they hold five to 10 times the potential learning power of a lecture or passive study.

So now we're ready for a step-by-step adventure into planning your own creative active-learning experiences.

Step 1: Form a planning team.

Many people fear designing their own programming because they feel insecure about their own creativity. We have a secret to share with you: People with big reputations for creativity often work with a team to produce ideas. Very few people develop creative programs in isolation. But when several people begin to toss ideas around, creativity blooms. Everyone possesses God-given creativity. Teamwork draws it out.

And a team offers a built-in refinement system for ideas. Team members build on each other's suggestions. Each person adds a new perspective to the process.

Planning teams should include young people as well as adults. Kids bring their own unique perspectives. Their fresh views can help you build more effective active-learning experiences. And rotating different kids onto your planning teams increases your young people's sense of ownership in the youth ministry. If they help plan it, they won't want to miss it. In addition, their learning will improve. People learn best when they participate in planning the learning activity.

You may find it helpful to schedule a monthly planning meeting. Your planners can lay out several weeks of active-learning experiences at one meeting.

Step 2: Select the topic.

Once you gather your team, decide what topic you wish to explore in an active-learning experience. Perhaps you'll choose peer pressure or forgiveness or premarital sex or communication with parents or the humanness of Jesus. You can base your topic on a scriptural truth or on your young people's current needs. For the latter you may wish to use results from a recent needs-evaluation survey.

One excellent tool you can use to survey your kids' needs is *Determining Needs in Your Youth Ministry* by Peter L. Benson and Dorothy L. Williams (Group Books). This resource supplies everything you need to conduct a comprehensive study: questionnaires, response sheets, tally charts and data-interpretation guides. The results of the survey may surprise you and will surely provide weeks of topic ideas.

Step 3: Articulate your message.

Let's say you discover that your teenagers need to develop better relationships with their parents. Specifically, they need to understand the need for forgiveness in family relationships. So you decide to use that as your topic.

Then determine what you'd like your students to learn about the topic. After discussing this with your team, reduce your learning objective to a single sentence. For example, "A good relationship with parents requires plenty of forgiveness."

You must confine your message to a "bite-size" morsel your kids can swallow. Many good learning activities turn sour when leaders try to accomplish too much in one session. Consider the topic chosen earlier. We know that building a good relationship with parents involves a lot more than forgiveness. But that one concept is plenty for young people to internalize in one sitting. They need to go away from the session saying, "Tonight I learned how important it is to forgive my parents and to ask for their forgiveness."

Simplifying your message to one sentence also helps you create the active-learning activity. You can design an experience around one simple concept far more easily than around an encyclopedia of teachings.

Step 4: Identify the empathy factor.

Look closely at your message sentence. What feeling dominates in this topic? That's the empathy factor. If you're dealing with forgiveness in the family, perhaps your key empathy factor is a sense of relief or freedom or restoration or love. You may choose to focus on a scripture passage, such as the parable of the prodigal son (Luke 15:11-32). The empathy factor brings difficult concepts down to a level that kids can understand.

You'll usually discover a number of appropriate empathy factors in any single message. Maybe you'll choose the desired positive feeling. Or perhaps you'll see more potential learning power in the negative emotion that often lurks within a topic. If you're studying cliques, for example, you could focus on the cold feeling of exclusion—or the warmth of inclusion. Perhaps your learning activity will provide opportunities to experience and contrast both feelings. Great!

Constructing learning activities around empathy factors makes good educational sense. Learning occurs when something impacts our inner being. And emotions serve as our internal impact instruments. For instance, we remember our visit to the Grand Canyon not because we read it was so many feet deep and so many miles long. We remember it because the feeling of awe sent tingles up our spines as we peered over the edge. Our emotions are our God-given internal cymbal crashes, drum rolls and violin strains.

Some people charge that using empathy factors crudely manipulates kids' feelings. It can, if misused. But properly applied, the use of empathy factors falls right in line with Jesus' example. He used the storm on the lake as an unforgettable active-learning experience for his disciples. Without the emotion of fear, that experience would've produced little lasting impact. Jesus knew that. And he used fear as an empathy factor—to teach.

Step 5: Devise an active way to evoke the empathy factor.

Now that you know your topic, your message and your empathy factor, create the action itself. Ask your planning team, "How can we immerse our young people in this empathy factor?" If you wish to evoke anger or forgiveness or restoration or love, how might you do that?

Use these guidelines as you consider different options in your planning:

● **Keep it active.** Remember, active-learning activities must involve everyone—actively. Avoid exercises that involve a couple of actors while everyone else passively watches.

● **Keep it physically and emotionally safe.** Stay away from activities that may place group members in danger—either physical or emotional. Never victimize a member in order to evoke the empathy factor. This includes simulations or role plays that attack individuals in the group. And avoid exercises that may cause embarrassment—such as games that unfairly disadvantage your overweight members. We once watched in horror as a pastor led junior highers in a mixer with the instruction, "Find the people in the room with the biggest feet, the longest nose and the biggest ears."

● **Incorporate an element of risk.** The best activities often have unpredictable outcomes. Your young people will sense this element of adventure, which will heighten their interest and draw out their creativity. And your debriefing time will generate much more interest and learning.

Your kids may say things like: "I had no idea Juan would walk out and leave the room during the clique game. But that's just like what happens in real life."

● **Keep it simple.** Too much complexity can work against you. Concentrate on creating the desired feelings. Then use the debriefing time to build on the message.

● **Use different approaches.** Consider a variety of different active-learning methods. Check out the list of possibilities on page 45.

Of course, you don't need to create all your active-learning experiences from scratch. The second half of this book offers a colorful selection of ready-to-go experiences. Use them. Adapt them. Modify them to meet your group's needs.

Scan the list of resources that starts on page 140. Those resources may inspire new ideas within you and your planning team.

Step 6: Do it.

Try your new experience in the group. If you've planned carefully, your young people will reap a significant learning experience. Even if your planned activity bombs, the active-learning process offers you an opportunity to debrief the failure. Your young people may learn even more from a bomb than from a perfectly executed activity.

Consider these pointers when leading active-learning experiences:

● **Be enthusiastic.** Your young people need to know that you believe in what you're doing. Especially when your kids aren't accustomed to active learning, they may grumble, "This is dumb." Just smile and say: "You may be right—but it's not the first time we've all done something dumb around here. Let's go! It'll be fun—dumb, but fun. Just think what fun you'll have explaining this to your mom when she asks what you did tonight."

● **Model vulnerability.** Active-learning experiences may fizzle if you model a "too cool" attitude. We've heard a

Active Ways to Learn

★ games

★ mixers

★ contrived experiences

★ simulation games

★ role plays

★ participatory skits (everyone involved)

★ clown ministry

★ readers' theater (choral reading)

★ arts and crafts

★ participatory music

★ recreational activities

★ group pantomimes

★ active case studies

★ creative writing

★ debates

★ mock trials

★ creative dance

★ charades

★ food preparation and eating

★ field trips

★ service projects

★ workcamps

★ adventure camping

★ stress courses (ropes, obstacle courses)

★ direct, purposeful experiences

number of youth leaders say, "That stuff may work for you but my kids are too mature for that juvenile approach." We've used—successfully—the ideas and experiences described in this book with thousands of teenagers, including legions of kids who thought they were too cool. No one outgrows the ability to learn and grow from active-learning experiences. In fact, you'll find similar success with these experiences when using them with all-adult groups.

● **Let other adults lead.** Especially if you feel uncomfortable leading a particular activity, ask other people to serve in leadership roles.

● **Involve young people in leadership.** They'll gain good experience, enhance their own learning and model enthusiastic involvement to their peers.

● **Participate in the experience.** Don't allow yourself or other adults to stand by passively. Only if your leadership duties prohibit you from joining the kids should you violate this basic rule.

Thom led a youth rally a few years ago that involved 300 kids and 100 adults. During every active-learning experience the adults sat passively on the gym bleachers as the kids eagerly participated on the floor. During debriefing, the adults had no idea what the kids were trying to express. The adults watched the activities but they missed the emotional impact because they refused to actively participate.

● **Be flexible.** If the experience falls through at some point, change and go with the unexpected. Always watch for teachable moments; they may come at any time.

● **Be a timekeeper.** Use your inner sense to know when to stop an activity. Don't allow games or other activities to run too long. Jump in and cut them off just before interest crests. Hone your timing skills: You want to leave your learners satisfied but yearning for more.

● **Be a coach.** Cheer your kids on: "That's great, Angie! Go for it, Bubba! Hang in there, Amy—you'll make it!" People learn best when teachers provide motivation and encouragement.

CHAPTER 6

Debriefing the Experience

So far we've examined the value of experience as an effective form of learning. But not all experiences result in wholesome education. Some experiences leave us with the wrong message. Others fail to teach us anything because we don't deliberately take the time to recognize, articulate and evaluate the inherent lessons.

Young people may share a stirring experience together. But they may never draw the rich Christian meaning from it unless we as leaders stop the action and help the kids interpret their experience.

Active learning takes on power when we reflect on an experience. We call this process debriefing. During debriefing we ask: "What just happened here? What can we learn from it? How will we be different because of it?"

Some young people learn without any debriefing. But debriefing as a group allows the students to verify their conclusions and measure them against other kids' perceptions. Debriefing takes advantage of peer influence. Some kids—after hearing their peers—say, "Yeah, that's just what I was thinking!" Others say, "Wow, I never thought about it like that!" Even rowdy kids who refuse to fully participate in the initial active-learning activity tend to sober up during the debriefing as they hear their peers sharing serious insights.

Before we dissect the debriefing process step by step, let's look at guidelines for the leader.

Guidelines for an active-learning leader

First, some good, freeing news: To lead active learning effectively, you don't have to be a dazzling speaker! Even if the mere idea of delivering a 30-minute youth talk turns your mouth to cotton, take heart. With gifts you already possess you can enable your young people to learn lifelong lessons. Use these guidelines to increase your effectiveness:

• **Understand how people learn.** Believe in active learning. Know that each individual learns at his or her own pace. Don't expect miracles; behavioral changes usually appear only gradually.

As a child, Vince experienced serious problems that now make relating to other people difficult for him. Although Vince has gone to church all his life, the other kids have never accepted him as a part of the group. But when Rick—the new youth minister—came, Vince began attending regularly and participating in all the activities.

To work on the problem between Vince and the other kids, Rick packs youth meetings with lots of active-learning times that center on strengthening relationships within the group. Even so, the other kids still don't reach out to Vince. Every youth meeting sets the stage for a silent tension between Vince and the other kids. Rick doesn't know how soon the lessons he's teaching will sink in. But he believes the situation will change through continued, patient guidance.

• **Expect learning to emerge at any time.** In active learning, fun times and serious times blur together. Bite your tongue if you start to say, "Okay everybody, the fun's over; now it's time to learn." Learning occurs during all phases of group experience—hilarious times, stressful times, frivolous times, quiet times. Be willing to debrief any meaningful happening at any time.

• **Be vulnerable.** If you're hesitant about sharing your own feelings, your young people will likely follow your lead. But if you open up and share your real self, your kids will do the same. Never ask young people to do something you're not willing to do yourself.

● **Use small groups.** Few people feel comfortable sharing personal information or feelings in front of a large audience. A feeling of intimacy enhances open discussion. If your group has more than eight people, divide it. Groups of four to six are ideal. Place a capable active-learning leader in each small group. Then after the groups debrief, ask a spokesperson from each small group to report highlights back to the large group. This builds community and enhances learning.

● **Share, don't railroad.** As the leader you need to share your own perspectives. But you don't need to campaign. You're one member of the group, with as much right to speak as anyone else. But you don't have the right to bulldoze a discussion and force-feed your views. Railroading doesn't teach, it alienates.

● **Let the kids have the final word.** When your young people discover good lessons through the debriefing process, fight the temptation to end the discussion with, "The *real* moral of the story is . . ." They learn more by discovering their own answers (with your help) than by hearing you deposit your knowledge into their brains.

● **Keep events moving.** In active learning, you act as the master of ceremonies. Keep the flow of events moving. Work to keep discussion interesting. Don't allow the action or the debriefing to bog down or drag out.

● **Learn from failures.** Help your kids see that we typically learn more from our failures than our successes. When something really bombs, rejoice! You have a wonderful teachable moment! Give your young people the freedom to fail.

● **Trust the Holy Spirit.** If you pray for the Holy Spirit to work within your young people during your active learning, then let him work! Believe that the great source of inspiration and insight isn't you—it's the Holy Spirit. Things may not go exactly as you planned. Kids may not draw the same messages from experiences as you do. Immerse your kids in quality experiences and allow God to touch them in unexpected ways.

● **Ask questions.** Question your kids instead of telling them all the answers. Students learn more when you ask them to find the answers. They learn less when the teacher merely hands out the answer sheet. Questions make learning more active for the student. Jesus, the master teacher, asked plenty of questions. To see the power of asking questions, check out the questions asked by Jesus in these passages:

Matthew 16:13	Luke 6:41-42
Matthew 22:42-45	Luke 7:42
Mark 4:21	John 6:5
Mark 4:40	John 13:12

Debriefing: a three-step process

Once your young people experience a significant activity, planned or serendipitous, you need to lead them through the debriefing process. Your kids will grow to expect you to say something like, "Hey, let's talk about what just happened here."

Debriefing promptly after the experience enhances learning greatly. If, after a morning experience, you wait until evening or the next day to debrief, the kids may forget some of the little details and feelings that erupted during the activity. Debrief when the experience is fresh.

Debriefing goes through three steps: reflection, interpretation and application.

1. Reflection—This first step asks the students: *How did you feel?* Our emotions tend to cement things into our memory. Think back to a junior high school teacher. What do you remember about him or her? Your memories probably strongly tie in to your emotions. Your teacher made you *feel* important or smart or dumb or indignant. Your feelings about that teacher fill a part of your personal history.

Ask your young people to name their feelings about

their experiences. Discussing feelings allows kids to venture past the mere statistics of the experience. Yes, Johnny may have just won the simulation game by snatching more tokens than anyone else, but how did that make everyone feel? Now you're entering a higher realm of learning.

Use open-ended questions to probe feelings. Avoid questions that kids can answer with a yes or no. "How did that make you feel?" is better than "Did that make you feel angry?" Let your kids know there are no wrong answers to your questions. Everyone's feelings are valid.

And in your small groups, ask everyone to share. We don't believe in announcing permission for group members to "pass" if they don't want to talk. That allows them to mentally check out of the discussion, to separate themselves from the other kids through their silence. Young people who participate in a youth ministry are members of a community—part of a family. They have an implied responsibility to function as members of the body. Your announcement of an unlimited right to pass is like a parent telling a child, "You never have to say anything in this family."

If a young person—on his or her own—asks to pass, you always have the option of honoring that particular request. You may know of circumstances in that teenager's life that would make his or her response too painful or inappropriate at that time.

Also, when probing feelings during debriefing, be prepared to hear some unexpected responses. It's normal for kids to experience feelings unlike any you're feeling. During a particular activity you may feel anger while the girl next to you feels sheer joy. Active learning allows (even celebrates) widely differing responses to the same learning experience.

2. Interpretation—The next step in the debriefing process asks: *What does this mean to you?* Now you're asking your young people to identify a message or principle from the experience. If your group has just locked arms and simulated a clique, your interpretation questions may include: "How is what we've just experienced like our youth group? What have we learned about that?"

Again, allow young people to discover the message themselves. Rather than telling kids the answer, take the time and ask questions to encourage self-discovery. Use scripture and discussion to explore how the actions and effects of their activity might translate to their lives.

Alert! Some of your kids may interpret wonderful messages you never intended. That's not failure! That's the Holy Spirit at work. God allows us to catch different glimpses of Jesus, even though we all may be looking through the same glass. God's Word speaks to each of us in a miraculously new and different way.

3. Application—The final debriefing step asks: *What will you do about it?* At this point your young people ask themselves: "What can I create with this new information? How can I make it a part of my life and use it?"

The learning now becomes internalized. It becomes a part of your young people. They've shared a common experience, taken information to a deep, personal, feeling level and discovered an important message. Now they must create something new with what they've experienced and interpreted. They must integrate the message into their lives.

The application stage of debriefing calls for commitment. Ask your young people how they'll change, how they'll grow, what they'll do as a result of your time together.

Too often we neglect commitment in the church. We may be diligent about selling our people on something, but we're timid about "closing the sale." We may robustly preach "love your neighbor," but we rarely ask individuals to pledge how they'll live out that Christian message next week.

Really, none of us accomplishes anything without commitment. If we want Christian growth in our young people, we must ask for their commitment.

The debriefing process creates a superb environment for commitment. We have witnesses! You see, commitments made without the scrutiny of witnesses typically get broken and forgotten. But witnesses provide accountability. We tend to say to ourselves, "I'd better follow through or those guys will find me out." Weight-loss parlors have made millions using this simple truth.

Within our small groups we can ask for commitment in many ways. We can call for oral commitment. Each young person can publicly answer a simple question, such as, "How will tonight's experience on cliques affect how you'll act in our group from now on?" or "Who's one person you'll call this week and invite to our group?"

Commitment can also come during prayer time, with each person asking aloud for God's help in accomplishing some goal.

And kids can write commitments in several different ways:

● Write a commitment on paper and exchange it with a partner. Then group members each pray for their partner's success.

● Make an individual commitment or sign a common commitment on a large sheet of newsprint.

● Write a commitment. The leader collects all the commitments and mails them back to the kids a month later as a motivating reminder.

CHAPTER 7

A Collection of Learning Experiences

I n this chapter, we've compiled 24 ready-to-use active-learning experiences to launch you toward more effective youth ministry. These activities can be used effectively in many different settings. Use them at retreats, Bible studies, youth meetings—even parties. Most of the activities can be used "as is" with any size group.

Although each activity is designed around a specific topic—such as friendship or forgiveness—each experience actually contains multiple themes. You can take each experience different directions, depending on how you debrief. For example, "The Colors of a Rainbow" demonstrates the importance of working together as parts of Christ's body. But by altering the debriefing questions, you can explore problems of racial prejudice and new ways of thinking about other ethnic groups.

To help you create alternate themes for each activity, we've set up an Index of Topics on page 144. The index lists themes directly covered by the activities, as well as themes you can examine by modifying the activities. Compose themes that your kids need to explore. Then use your own creativity to modify these activities—or design your own—to help kids learn more about their lives and their faith. Enjoy!

When Putdowns Tear Down

Purpose
To demonstrate the damage of putdowns

Materials
For every six people:
- paper cutout person
- 6 inches of masking tape

For each person:
- pencil
- 3×5 card

Optional:
- newsprint
- markers

Action
Form circles with groups no larger than six. Give each group a paper person. Say: Imagine your paper cutout is a real person. The person holding the paper person will start the activity. That person must say a putdown (such as, "You're stupid" or "You dress weird") and rip off a portion of the paper person's body. That person then passes the paper person to the right. The next person does the same: says a putdown, tears off part of the paper person and passes it along. Continue around the circle until I say stop.

Make sure the paper person in each circle makes it around at least once. Then call a halt to the putdowns.

Read aloud Ephesians 4:29: "Do not let any unwholesome talk come out of your mouths, but only what is helpful for building others up according to their needs, that it may benefit those who listen."

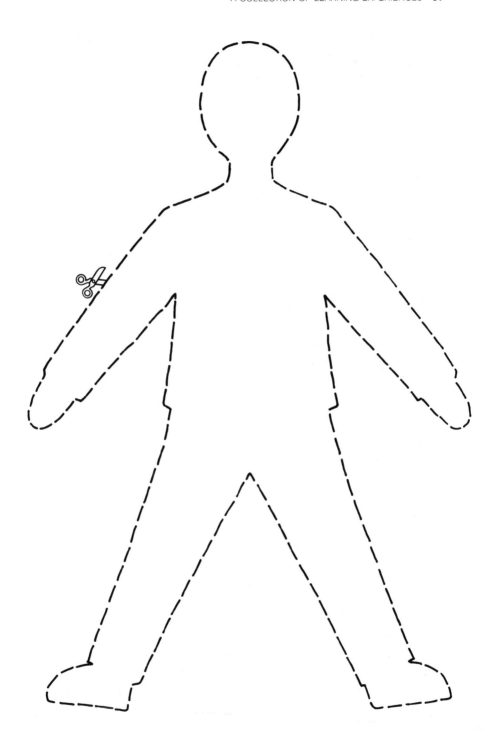

Instruct each group to pass around its paper person once again. Only this time kids each must say a kind, loving word while they use a piece of tape to reconstruct the paper person.

After young people have pieced together the paper person, have them place it in the center of their group.

Reflection

In their groups, have kids each respond to these questions:

● How did you feel as you said the putdown and tore the person apart? (Some may say, "Terrible" or "It was fun!")

● How did you feel as you gave a kind word and taped the person back together? (Some may say, "Good" or "It was harder to think of good words; it was easier to clown around with putdowns.")

● Which did you feel was easier to do—put down or build up? Why? (Some may say, "It was easier to give putdowns because they felt like jokes" or "The good words were easier for me because I don't like to hurt people.")

Interpretation

In their groups, have kids each respond to these questions:

● How was this experience like what we do to people in real life? (Some may say, "We put down people without thinking of the damage we might do" or "Good words can really heal someone.")

● Compare what happened to the paper person with what happens to real people. (Some may say, "Putdowns hurt" or "We can't undo the harm without leaving some scars.")

Application

Have kids each think of someone they know who could use a kind word, someone who needs to be built up. Say:

Write that person's name on a 3×5 card. Then write what you plan to tell that person and when you plan to do that.

Have kids share their plans with their small group.

Tell young people to write their name, address and phone number on the back of their 3×5 card. Then have them exchange cards. Encourage group members to hold each other accountable to their promises by calling or dropping reminder notes during the next week. Also invite kids to pray that compassion and love shows through the person whose address is written on the card.

For further follow-up, make a newsprint banner decorated with the words, "Do not let any unwholesome talk come out of your mouths . . ." (Ephesians 4:29a). Attach the paper persons to the banner as a reminder of the damage that put-downs deliver.

Casting the First Stone

Purpose

To show the danger of "rock throwing" (putdowns)

Materials

For every six people:
- one foam-rubber "rock" (Purchase in magic or novelty shops. Or order from Edmund Scientific, 101 East Gloucester Pike, Barrington, NJ 08007.)

Action

Form circles of up to six people. Find out whose birthday in each circle falls closest to Christmas. Have that person stand in the center of the circle. Instruct the other group members to imagine the person in the center is someone of the opposite sex. So if Joe is in the center, kids picture Joe as a girl; if Christine is in the center, they imagine her as a guy. Have group members think of putdowns commonly thrown at someone of that sex. For example, putdowns tossed at guys might be "dumb jock" or "nerd"; putdowns tossed at girls might be "loose" or "air head." (This is important: Kids must imagine the opposite sex so the putdowns can't be made directly to the person in the center.)

Hand a foam-rubber "rock" to someone in each group. Ask kids each to shout a putdown as they throw the rock at the person in the center. After one person throws the rock, anyone else in the circle may pick it up and throw it. Allow a few minutes for the kids to throw stones (putdowns).

Stop the activity and ask everyone to sit down.

Reflection

In their groups, have kids each respond to these questions:

● How did you feel when you first heard the instructions and saw the rock? (Some may say, "I didn't like the idea of throwing something at someone" or "This will be fun.")

● How did you feel being the stone throwers? (Some may say, "I was glad I wasn't in the middle" or "It was kind of fun.")

● How did you feel being the person getting "stoned"? (Some may say, "I was afraid" or "I didn't like it.")

Interpretation

In their groups, have kids each respond to these questions:

● How is this experience like real life? (Some may say, "It's fun to join in with a group to go after somebody" or "Putdowns thrown in fun can really hurt someone.")

● Are you more often the putdown thrower or the one who receives all the putdowns? Explain. (Some may say, "I get involved in making fun of people because I don't want to go against the crowd" or "I feel like I'm the one everybody picks on because I'm shy and can't stand up to their attacks.")

● Why do people throw stones? (Some may say, "They want to build themselves up by putting others down" or "Some kids aren't serious and just think they're being funny.")

Application

Set up the scripture reading by saying: Throwing stones is serious business. It really can hurt someone. Pass the rock around the group from person to person as I read from John 8. I'll pause after each verse to allow time for you to pass the rock to the next person. Use the silence as a solemn time to reflect on any putdowns you may have thrown in the past.

"The teachers of the law and the Pharisees brought in a woman caught in adultery. They made her stand before the group . . ."

(Pause)

"and said to Jesus, 'Teacher, this woman was caught in the act of adultery.' "

(Pause)

" 'In the Law Moses commanded us to stone such women. Now what do you say?' "

(Pause)

"They were using this question as a trap, in order to have a basis for accusing him. But Jesus bent down and started to write on the ground with his finger."

(Pause)

"When they kept on questioning him, he straightened up and said to them, 'If any one of you is without sin, let him be the first to throw a stone at her.' "

(Pause)

"Again he stooped down and wrote on the ground. At this, those who heard began to go away one at a time, the older ones first,"

(Pause)

"until only Jesus was left, with the woman still standing there. Jesus straightened up and asked her, 'Woman, where are they? Has no one condemned you?' "

(Pause)

" 'No one, sir,' she said. 'Then neither do I condemn you,' Jesus declared. 'Go now and leave your life of sin' " (John 8:3-11).

After the reading, allow time for further discussion. Then conclude with prayer. Have kids pass the rock around the circle. As kids each receive the rock, have them offer a sentence prayer.

Or Try This

For an alternative, upbeat conclusion to this learning activity, use the Action section from "You Are the Light of the World," on page 122. Instead of using a candle or Cyalume stick, have kids pass the rock to each other.

Refer to Jesus as the "Rock" (Psalm 18:2; 19:14). Say: Instead of hurling putdowns we can show people Jesus, the Rock, through our words and actions.

The Colors of a Rainbow

Purpose

To celebrate the uniqueness that each person brings to the body of Christ

Materials

For each person:
- one sheet of construction paper (These six colors must be represented: red, orange, yellow, green, blue, violet.)
- pencil

Action

Distribute the six colors of construction paper among the group. Explain that everyone will help *do* the scripture reading from 1 Corinthians 12. Have the kids practice the parts as you call out one color at a time. When kids hear their color, have them raise their construction paper in the air and wave it. When you say the word "rainbow," have all the young people wave their construction paper colors.

Read the following paraphrase of 1 Corinthians 12:

A Rainbow Reading

Christ is like a single **rainbow** which has many colors: **red, orange, yellow, blue, green, violet**. It's still one **rainbow**, even though it's made up of different colors.

For the **rainbow** itself isn't made up of only one

color like **red** or **green**, but it's made up of many colors.

If **yellow** were to say, "Because I'm not ~~violet~~ blue, I don't belong to the **rainbow**," that wouldn't keep it from being a color of the **rainbow**. If the whole **rainbow** were only **orange**, how could it be as beautiful? And if it were only **blue**, how could it show up in the sky?

As it is, however, God put every different color in the **rainbow** just as he wanted it to be. It wouldn't be a **rainbow** if it were only **violet**—or **yellow**—or **red**—or **blue**—or **green**—or **orange**.

As it is, there are many colors, but one **rainbow**.

All of you are Christ's **rainbow**—and each one of you is a special color in it!

Reflection

Have kids form groups of six by collecting one person with each color. Groups each should contain the six colors.

In their groups, have kids each respond to these questions:

● How did you feel when your color was called? (Some may say, "Silly and self-conscious" or "I felt like I had something to contribute.")

● How did you feel when someone else's color was called? (Some may say, "It was fun to watch the colors appear" or "I kept wanting my color to be called.")

Interpretation

In their groups, have kids each respond to these questions:

● How would you compare those feelings to how you feel about sharing your God-given gifts and abilities? (Some may say, "I feel self-conscious" or "I get excited and feel proud.")

• What does this passage say about uniqueness and how we work together as a body? (Some may say, "It shows the beauty of working together" or "We need each other.")

• What's good about being unique? (Some may say, "That means you're very special" or "You're created for a purpose.")

• What's difficult about being unique? (Some may say, "People might think you're weird" or "You have to be more responsible.")

Application

Instruct kids each to write their name on the top of their construction paper and pass it around to the others in their group. Have each person write a talent, gift or quality demonstrated by the person whose name appears at the top of the paper.

When the paper returns to its owner, have each person first read the list silently. Then have kids each make a spoken commitment by reading the list aloud, only adding someone or a group who could benefit from each gift. For example, if the list said, "always has a smile," the person might say, "I promise to give my brother Roger a smile instead of a scowl all the time."

Continue around the circle until each person has stated a promise for each gift.

Or Try This

You can also use this activity to encourage racial equality and discourage prejudice in your group. Do all the exercises as written. When you get to the Interpretation section, ask the kids:

• How would you compare those feelings to how different ethnic groups feel about their heritage? (Some may say, "They may feel they're overlooked" or "They're proud of their heritage.")

● What does this passage say about different ethnic groups working together? (Some may say, "We're all needed to make the picture complete" or "There's a lot of tension because everyone wants center stage.")

● What's good about having multiple, unique, ethnic groups? (Some may say, "We can learn from each other" or "It makes life more interesting.")

● What's difficult about having multiple, unique, ethnic groups? (Some may say, "Prejudice" or "Conflicting cultural values.")

For the Application section, have kids each share their ethnic heritage with the other members in their group. (If some kids don't know their heritage, have them team up with another group member and agree to research their family trees and report their findings to each other within the next week.)

Have the groups sit in circles. Tell kids to go around the circle and each offer a sentence prayer about prejudice in their own lives or in the world. After each prayer, have that person toss his or her construction paper into the circle's center, creating a "rainbow" of prayer.

What Did You Notice?

. . . .

Purpose

To see whether people really notice the "little things" about others

Materials

- newsprint
- markers

Action

Have people pair up and sit facing each other knee to knee. Allow a few minutes for conversation. Suggest they discuss the highlights—and the lowlights—of the past week.

Call time and have partners sit back to back. Say: Change something about your appearance that you think your partner won't notice. For example, untie a shoe, take off your watch, change your hair style, whatever!

Give twosomes time to make the changes. Then have each person turn and face his or her partner. Have the partners try to detect the change.

Reflection

In pairs, have kids each respond to this question:
- How did you feel about being "discovered"—or not being discovered? (Some may say, "She didn't even notice!" or "I couldn't believe he spotted that tiny change!")

Interpretation

In pairs, have kids each respond to these questions:

● How is this experiment like real life when it comes to getting noticed? (Some may say, "The days I don't want to go to school because I feel like everyone will see the big zit on my chin—maybe other people don't even notice it" or "I like it when people notice the little things that I do for them.")

● Do you want people to notice the little things about you? Why or why not? (Some may say, "No! I feel so self-conscious that I hate to think of people looking at me" or "Yeah, I want people to know I exist. I want to be remembered.")

● What are you most self-conscious about other people noticing? (Some may say, "After eating I'm afraid I might have food stuck in my teeth or plastered on my face" or "I'm self-conscious about wearing the 'right' or 'wrong' clothes.")

● What do you *want* people to notice about you? (Some may say, "I'd like people to notice the nice stuff I do for them" or "I like it when somebody thinks I've got a good sense of humor.")

Application

As a large group, have the kids brainstorm and list on newsprint ideas under these four categories:

1. When self-consciousness is good (Some may say, "When you want to brush your teeth and use deodorant!" or "When you're concerned about respecting others.")

2. When self-consciousness is harmful (Some may say, "When it makes me hate myself" or "When my own self-centeredness keeps me from reaching out to others.")

3. When wanting to be noticed is good (Some may say, "When I've worked hard for something" or "When you're witnessing your faith.")

4. When wanting to be noticed is harmful (Some may say, "When you're being rowdy and disrupting a group" or "When you think you're so cool and want to show off.")

Have kids get back with their partners, then each choose from the list one area they need to work on most and tell their partner.

Wrap up by having partners close their eyes and join hands while you read verses from Psalm 139.

Psalm 139:1-6, 13-16, 23-24

O Lord, you have searched me and you know me.

You know when I sit and when I rise; you perceive my thoughts from afar.

You discern my going out and my lying down; you are familiar with all my ways.

Before a word is on my tongue you know it completely, O Lord.

You hem me in—behind and before; you have laid your hand upon me.

Such knowledge is too wonderful for me, too lofty for me to attain.

For you created my inmost being; you knit me together in my mother's womb.

I praise you because I am fearfully and wonderfully made; your works are wonderful, I know that full well.

My frame was not hidden from you when I was made in the secret place. When I was woven together in the depths of the earth,

your eyes saw my unformed body. All the days ordained for me were written in your book before one of them came to be.

Search me, O God, and know my heart; test me and know my anxious thoughts.

See if there is any offensive way in me, and lead me in the way everlasting.

Reconciliation

Purpose

To experience separation and reconciliation

Materials

For each person:
- Bible
- 3×5 card
- pencil

Action

Have group members form a circle. (This can be done in one large group if the room permits, otherwise form groups of six to eight people.) Have people place their arms around each other as you say: This experience may seem uncomfortable and you may even feel like laughing at times. But please use this as a worshipful time to experience what can happen to us as God's people.

Say: Being a part of a group can be lots of fun because we can enjoy the feeling of togetherness. But it doesn't always work that way.

Pause for a moment. Then continue with this experience:

Say: Sometimes we separate ourselves from each other and can't enjoy the love God intends for us. (Short pause)

If you have been part of a group and have ever let that group down, I'd like you to drop your arms to your sides. (Pause)

Sometimes we say things that are harmful to other people. (Short pause)

I'd like anyone who's ever said something harmful to

another member of a group to take a step backward. (Pause)

Often we exclude others from our group. (Short pause)

If anyone has ever excluded another person from a group or made someone feel left out, please take a step backward. (Pause)

Sometimes we say things that aren't true. We deny making a mistake, or we're afraid to tell somebody something. (Short pause)

If this has ever happened to you, I'd like you to turn and face away from the center of the circle. (Pause)

Sometimes we pretend not to see the needs of other people. (Short pause)

If there have been times you've ignored the needs of others and remained apart from them, I'd like you to close your eyes and keep them closed. (Pause)

We're meant to be together, yet at times our actions keep us apart. (Short pause)

If you've ever helped someone with a need, I'd like you to turn around. (Pause)

It's important to listen to people. (Short pause)

If you've ever taken the time to listen to a friend who had a problem, I'd like you to take one step in. (Pause)

We build people up when we welcome them and make them feel included. (Short pause)

If you've ever made someone feel welcome and a part of things, open your eyes. (Pause)

Confession to one another can tear down walls. (Short pause)

If you've ever shared a way that you failed someone, even if it was hard to do, take another step in. (Pause)

God asks us to forgive one another. (Short pause)

If you've ever forgiven someone, place your arms around the people beside you.

Suggest the kids give each other a group hug.

Reflection

Form groups of six to eight. In their groups, have kids

each respond to these questions:

● How did you feel during the first half of the experience? (Some may say, "Self-conscious" or "I felt okay when I realized I wasn't the only one who'd blown it.")

● How did you feel during the second half of the experience? (Some may say, "I felt relieved" or "It felt warm and cozy to be back together again.")

Interpretation

In their groups, have kids each respond to these questions:

● How is this experience like what happens in our relationships with other people? (Some may say, "The dumb stuff we do does stand in the way sometimes" or "Admitting a mistake might bring me and my mom together.")

● What actions and words separate you from others? (Some may say, "When people don't talk to me at youth group" or "When I talk about people behind their backs.")

● What actions and words bring people together? (Some may say, "Praise" or "When someone smiles and says 'hi' to me in the hall.")

Application

Make sure everyone has a Bible. Have kids look up Galatians 5:19-21. As a group, have them think of examples at school, home, work and in the world that illustrate the passage.

Next have them read Galatians 5:22-25. Encourage kids each to choose one fruit of the Spirit to put into action this week—one that will bring them closer to someone. Have kids each write that fruit on a 3×5 card and write the way they'll put it into action. For example: "Patience: I'll be more patient with my little sister by not yelling at her and by letting her borrow my tapes."

The experience in the Action section is reprinted from *The Giving Book* by Paul M. Thompson and Joani Schultz. Copyright John Knox Press 1985. Used by permission of Westminister/John Knox Press.

Wall-Makers and Wall-Breakers

Purpose

To experience how forgiveness breaks down walls caused by sin

Materials

- stacks of newspapers
- masking tape
- garbage bags

Action

Form groups no larger than six. (A group can be just two people.) Tell groups they each must build a wall to hide their group from the other groups. Give them newspapers and masking tape. Suggest making paper tubes for bars or taping sheets of newspapers together to create curtains or walls. Tell groups they must remain in the meeting room, but they can creatively use anything in the room to help; for example, chairs, walls, tables. Encourage them to see who can best hide from the rest.

Once groups are behind their "walls," say: We're going to discover and experience the joy of forgiveness. But before we can celebrate, we must recognize our shortcomings and failures as God's people. Sin separates. Walls of sin can keep us from relationships that could be. For the next few moments, imagine that the walls you've created are walls that alienate you and keep you from each other.

Have each group choose one "wall-maker" that separates one person from another. Examples include: cheating, hating, cussing, lying, boasting, stealing. When each group has selected a wall-maker, choose one person to be in an open space between the groups to speak the "wall-breaker" word: forgiven.

Have the person in the open space softly say "forgiven" again and again. Serve as "choral director" and, one by one, cue the groups behind the walls by tapping on their walls to designate when to start shouting the wall-maker. Bit by bit the sounds of sin will appear to cover up "forgiven," yet all the while "forgiven" continues to be spoken. The wall-makers will gradually become louder. Then reverse the chants' volume by eliminating the wall-maker chanting, one by one, until "forgiven" is the final word that is heard.

Read aloud Ephesians 2:14: "For he himself is our peace, who has made the two one and has destroyed the barrier, the dividing wall of hostility."

Say: Christ is the ultimate wall-breaker. Let's rejoice that we're the ones God uses today as wall-breakers. God speaks the good word of forgiveness through each of us.

Have everyone celebrate by tearing down the newspaper walls and stuffing them into garbage bags. Set the garbage bags aside for later use.

Reflection

In their groups, have kids each respond to these questions:

● How did you feel when you started building the walls? (Some may say, "It was a lot of fun!" or "I liked the idea of our little group being separate.")

● How did you feel after you'd been behind your wall for a while? (Some may say, "It was fun at first, but then it got stuffy and hot" or "I couldn't wait to get out of there.")

● How did it feel when you got to tear down the walls? (Some may say, "Great!" or "It was so freeing.")

Interpretation

In their groups, have kids each respond to these questions:

● How is this experience like the separation sin causes? (Some may say, "At first, some of the bad stuff we get into seems fun, but after a while, it can start to suffocate us" or "The sin in our lives keeps us from being honest and out in the open with others.")

● How did this experience demonstrate forgiveness? (Some may say, "It's like a breath of fresh air" or "It allows you to reach out and associate with others more freely.")

● How is forgiveness in our lives similar to the speaking of "forgiven" during the shouting? (Some may ask, "The word 'forgiven' was being spoken too?" or say, "Forgiveness is available to us through Jesus, but we don't take advantage of it.")

Application

Give each person a page of a newspaper. Say: This newspaper will represent a wall-maker in your life—something that separates you from enjoying the love of God or the love of others.

Have kids each hold their paper while telling the small group about a wall-maker that's been a painful part of their life. Encourage young people to share times they felt separated from others by sin.

After each person shares, have the other group members offer that person words of forgiveness and care. Suggest a few phrases or words, such as "God loves you and forgives you" and "We forgive you and so does God." As kids each receive the words of forgiveness, have them crumple the newspaper and stuff it in a garbage bag.

For fun, celebrate the joy of forgiveness and freedom from all the "garbage" by playing volleyball with the full garbage bags!

The Ins and Outs of Cliques

Purpose

To experience the pain and pleasure of cliques

Materials

- newsprint
- markers

Action

Form circles of groups no larger than eight. Have each group find out whose full name has the most letters in it. Then have that person step outside the circle. Instruct the groups each to keep the "outsider" out of their circle. Tell the outsiders each to use any means possible to get into the circle.

If time allows, give different people the opportunity to try to break in.

Reflection

In their groups, have kids each respond to these questions:

- How did it feel being in the "in" crowd? (Some may say, "It was great!" or "I felt sorry for the person on the outside.")
- How did it feel being the person trying to break in? (Some may say, "I felt like giving up" or "I thought it was a fun challenge.")

Interpretation

In their groups, have kids each respond to these questions:

● How is this experience like cliques at school? at youth group? (Some may say, "Being on the inside circle, I hardly even noticed somebody was out there. That's a lot like our youth group." Or "I wanted to let her in, but the rest of the group didn't. It was just like the pressure at school to not include somebody who's not 'acceptable.' ")

● What do cliques do to keep people out? (Some may say, "They plan parties and make sure certain people aren't invited" or "Some cliques have requirements—like money, the right clothes or doing drugs.")

● What do people do to fit in, to become accepted in a group? (Some may say, "Some give up their values and morals" or "Some kids pretend to be somebody they're not just to fit in.")

Application

In their groups, have kids each respond to these questions:

● What about our youth group? What have we done to make people belong and feel welcome? (Some may say, "We have 'Bring a Friend Night' so new people can get used to us" or "Manuel and Sarah are great talking to newcomers and helping them join in.")

● What has our youth group done to exclude people? (Some may say, "We like being together so much that when new people come, we sometimes ignore them" or "We break up into school groups because we feel most comfortable with those people.")

Read aloud Romans 15:5-7. As a large group, brainstorm and list on newsprint ways your youth group can be more sensitive to the lonely, shy or new people who might not feel they fit in. For example, designate greeters, plan a buddy system or play get-acquainted games at every meeting so group members can learn more about each other.

Combine similar ideas. Have the kids rank them and choose at least two favorites your group will put into practice.

Have an artistic young person recopy the list to be hung in a prominent place where the youth group meets.

Have the group join hands in one large circle. Pray for God's help in accepting others and putting the ideas into practice.

Go, Team, Go!

■ ■

Purpose

To experience the joy and frustration of working together

Materials

For every six people:

- six different-shape "tossable" objects from home or around the meeting room (for example, a football, Frisbee, drinking straw, can of soup, sock, a pingpong ball, keys, purse, pencil)

Action

Form groups of six people, standing. Make sure each person has an object to toss. Then have people in each small group hand their objects to one person in their group. This person lays the objects in a pile on the floor and chooses the first object to toss. He or she tosses the object to one person in the group who catches and tosses it to another. Each person in the group must receive and toss the object until it returns to the original person. Groups must set up a pattern for tossing each object. (The only pattern not allowed is simply going around the circle from right to left or left to right.)

Have each group practice juggling the one object in its pattern. Once everyone has that down, the person with all the objects adds another object to the tossing pattern. The point? To eventually "group juggle" all the objects at the same time.

Reflection

In their groups, have kids each respond to these questions:

● How did you feel when only one object was being tossed? (Some may say, "It was fun and easy" or "I felt like it wasn't a challenge.")

● How did you feel when all the objects were being tossed? (Some may say, "It frustrated me because we kept dropping them" or "I liked the challenge and the way we worked together.")

Interpretation

In their groups, have kids each respond to these questions:

● How is this experience like working together in a group? (Some may say, "Everybody had to do their part to make it work" or "If we don't have a plan things can really fall apart.")

● What's helpful about working as a team? (Some may say, "None of us could've juggled all those things alone, but a group can" or "It's more fun than doing things all by yourself.")

● What's frustrating about working as a team? (Some may say, "If one person doesn't do his or her part, everything can fall apart" or "It can be stressful if you're not trying to accomplish the same goal.")

● How is this like our youth group working together? (Some may say, "Our youth group doesn't seem to have a common goal so sometimes things fall apart" or "We're trying to do a lot of projects—like tossing a lot of objects—but nothing's organized.")

Application

In their groups, have kids each respond to these questions:

● In what ways do our youth group members work together well? (Some may say, "We all contribute good ideas" or "We like to be together.")

● How could we improve the way we work together? (Some may say, "We need to get organized" or "We need to recognize the value of each person's contribution to the group.")

Have each group decide which of its objects best represents the youth group right now and explain why to the rest of the groups. Then in each small group, have the person who started the tossing pattern earlier hold the object and say what he or she will do to build team spirit. (For example, "I'll promise to really make the phone calls when I say I will" or "I'd like to volunteer for a planning committee to help get our group better organized.") Then have the person toss the object to the next person in the pattern and have him or her make a promise. Continue until the object makes it around the circle once.

Have a young person read aloud Philippians 1:3-6, 9-11: "I thank my God every time I remember you. In all my prayers for all of you, I always pray with joy because of your partnership in the gospel from the first day until now, being confident of this, that he who began a good work in you will carry it on to completion until the day of Christ Jesus. And this is my prayer: that your love may abound more and more in knowledge and depth of insight, so that you may be able to discern what is best and may be pure and blameless until the day of Christ, filled with the fruit of righteousness that comes through Jesus Christ—to the glory and praise of God."

Instruct the groups each to toss an object around their circle again. Have each person say a prayer of thanks for the person who just tossed the object. Have them continue around the circle until each person has been prayed for.

Building Together

· ·

Purpose

To understand the importance of teamwork

Materials

For every six people:
- four ounces of uncooked spaghetti
- 10 gumdrops

Action

Form groups no larger than six. Give each group 10 gumdrops and four ounces of uncooked spaghetti. Say: Build the best tower you can with your building materials of gumdrops and spaghetti. There's one catch: no talking.

Allow 10 to 15 minutes for tower-building. Then call time and praise the creativity and ingenuity of the construction crews.

Reflection

In their groups, have kids each respond to these questions:

- How did you feel during the construction of the tower? (Some may say, "I got frustrated because the spaghetti kept breaking" or "I felt really proud of how our group designed the tower.")
- How did you feel about not being able to speak? (Some may say, "I wanted to give instructions and didn't know how to communicate without speaking" or "I enjoyed how we devised creative ways to get our points across.")

Interpretation

In their groups, have kids each respond to these questions:

● How is this experience like how our youth group works together? (Some may say, "We can come up with some pretty incredible stuff when we put our minds to it!" or "We had trouble with nobody taking any leadership.")

● Were you more of a leader or a follower? Explain. (Some may say, "I liked to sit back and let other people do the work" or "I liked to be in charge and get people going.")

● What role did each person play during the construction process? How is that like or unlike the way he or she normally responds in the youth group? (Some may say, "Dave had great ideas for the tower, but in our group he usually holds back his ideas" or "Jenny was the cheerleader for our tower-building by clapping when it held together. She's our youth group encourager and cheerleader too.")

● Were you satisfied with how your group worked together? Why or why not? (Some may say, "Yes! We rallied together and created a work of art!" Or "No. Only two people really built the tower. The rest of the group just watched.")

Application

Have each person tell the whole group one thing he or she would like to improve when it comes to teamwork. (For example, "I want to be a better listener" or "I want to jump in with my ideas and not be afraid of what others think.")

Have kids join hands in a circle. Read aloud Ephesians 4:7, 12-13. Conclude by having kids each say a prayer for the person on their right. The prayer can include an encouraging request for improvement or a word of thanks for that person's special contribution to the group.

For fun, join all the towers together and make a mega-tower! Here's a hint: Build it in a space where it can stand for a while without needing to be moved. Let the group admire it for a few weeks.

A Miracle Meal

Purpose

To experience community and God's grace

Materials

- one dinner roll or doughnut

Action

Say: Sometimes we feel inadequate. We don't think we're good enough. We feel we don't have what it takes. We sometimes doubt that God will provide what we need. The disciples felt like this when they were faced with feeding more than 5,000 people.

Read aloud Matthew 14:15-21:

"As evening approached, the disciples came to him and said, 'This is a remote place, and it's already getting late. Send the crowds away, so they can go to the villages and buy themselves some food.'

"Jesus replied, 'They do not need to go away. You give them something to eat.'

" 'We have here only five loaves of bread and two fish,' they answered.

" 'Bring them here to me,' he said. And he directed the people to sit down on the grass. Taking the five loaves and two fish and looking up to heaven, he gave thanks and broke the loaves. Then he gave them to the disciples, and the disciples gave them to the people. They all ate and were satisfied, and the disciples picked up 12 basketfuls of broken pieces that were left over. The number of those who ate was about 5,000 men, besides women and children."

Then say: In the same way, we'll now share in a meal. I

believe there will be enough for each of us. After the bread has been distributed, we shall all eat at once.

For groups of 50 or fewer, hold up the dinner roll or doughnut and tear off a small piece (about one-fourth). Use the small piece to "feed" the group. Silently break it into three or four smaller pieces and distribute them among the group. (If your group has 50 to 200 people, use half the roll or doughnut. A single roll or doughnut may be used—believe it or not—for groups of 200 to 500.)

Quietly wait until the people "catch on" to share the pieces with each other.

Once everyone has received a small piece, say, Let's share in this meal together.

Eat, then hold out your hand to collect any leftovers. Hold up the remaining dinner roll or doughnut and the leftovers for all to see.

Reflection

In their groups, have kids each respond to these questions:

● How did you feel when you saw what we were all going to eat? (Some may say, "I felt it was impossible" or "I wondered what was going on.")

● How did you feel when just a small portion was distributed? (Some may say, "I thought I might not get any" or "I didn't understand what was happening.")

● How did you feel when the bread was shared around the group? (Some may say, "I got one of the first pieces and didn't know what I was supposed to do with it" or "I wanted to make sure everyone got something even if it was small.")

● How did you feel when we ate the bread? (Some may say, "I felt a spirit of communion with the group" or "I thought my piece was so small that I wouldn't be able to taste it, but I could! And it was good!")

Interpretation

In their groups, have kids each respond to these questions:

● How is this experience like a miracle? (Some may say, "I didn't think it could be done, but it happened!" or "It took trust that there'd be enough for everybody.")

● What did God teach you through this experience? (Some may say, "It's important to look out for each other's interests, and when we do, there's plenty for all" or "I sometimes feel like I have nothing to offer, but even my little bit can make a difference.")

Application

Tell young people to pair up. Have them tell their partners one way they will allow God to "break" them and use them to meet needs in their families, friendships, church and the world.

Have partners pray for each other. Challenge them to become prayer partners for a designated time period (one week, six weeks or six months) so they can support each other as they work their "miracles."

Or Try This

This activity also works great as a combination communion service and meeting on world hunger. Carry out the activity as described. Then during the Application section, pass out pamphlets from your denomination's hunger relief organization or another reputable hunger relief organization. (Be sure you research them carefully!) Compassion International is one good choice. To receive a supply of pamphlets, send a letter of request to:

Compassion International
3955 Cragwood Drive
Box 7000
Colorado Springs, CO 80933

Discuss how even the little we give can go a long way

toward helping those in need. Suggest that one way we can make our "little" grow to "a lot" is by sponsoring a child overseas. After reviewing the information with the kids, have the group vote on whether as a team to sponsor one or more children.

If the group votes "yes," designate a group member to act as the coordinator. He or she will be responsible to collect money every month and mail it to the relief organization. Also assign several kids to write letters periodically to the sponsored child. You may even want to take a group photograph to send with one of the letters. Include the group members' names on the back.

Fishers of Men (and Women!)

Purpose

To explore what it means to be a witness

Materials

- large, strong net at least 4×6 feet (standard types available in most army surplus stores)

For each person:

- string
- pencil
- construction paper fish with a hole punched in it

Action

Lay the net in the middle of the room. Ask for a volunteer to lie on top of the net. Then ask another volunteer to lift that person using the net. After a few attempts, encourage more and more people to help. If you have a large group, you can add another person in the net.

Make sure group members keep safety in mind as they lift the people in the net. Have lots of fun—and laughs.

Reflection

Form groups of three. In their groups, have kids each respond to this question:

- How did you feel during this experience? (Some may say, "I tried to lift the person in the net and felt helpless because I needed more strength" or "I felt proud that as we all worked together, we could lift the people in the net.")

Interpretation

Read aloud Mark 1:14-20: "After John was put in prison, Jesus went into Galilee, proclaiming the good news of God.

" 'The time has come,' he said. 'The kingdom of God is near. Repent and believe the good news!'

"As Jesus walked beside the Sea of Galilee, he saw Simon and his brother Andrew casting a net into the lake, for they were fishermen.

" 'Come, follow me,' Jesus said, 'and I will make you fishers of men.'

"At once they left their nets and followed him. When he had gone a little farther, he saw James son of Zebedee and his brother John in a boat, preparing their nets. Without delay he called them, and they left their father Zebedee in the boat with the hired men and followed him."

In their groups, have kids each respond to these questions:

● How was our "net experience" like being "fishers of men"? (Some may say, "A lot of us hesitated to get involved and that's how I feel sometimes when it comes to witnessing" or "Being a 'fisher of men' is easier when you know you've got support and help all around you.")

● How do your feelings about being a Christian witness compare to the early disciples? (Some may say, "I don't like the thought of leaving behind the things that have been important to me—even if they stand in the way" or "The first disciples must have felt shocked; I do too, thinking that God wants *me* to share the good news.")

● How does this experience demonstrate our need for others? (Some may say, "When you have problems, you usually can't solve them without support from others" or "Lots of times I want to make it on my own, but that's when I should welcome others' help.")

Application

Give each person string, a pencil and a construction paper fish. Have kids each write on their fish the name of someone with whom they want to share the "good news" from God. In their groups of three, have young people tell about the person on the fish. Have them explain what they plan to say and do to witness in a special way to that person. Encourage trios to pray for each other throughout the week.

Tell the kids each to put the string through their fish.

Then read aloud Mark 1:16: "As Jesus walked beside the Sea of Galilee, he saw Simon and his brother Andrew casting a net into the lake, for they were fishermen." Pause, and instruct two people to come toward the net.

Continue by reading Mark 1:17: "Come, follow me . . . and I will make you fishers of men [and women]." Ask the two to tie their construction paper fish to the net. Then have them bring two more people to tie their fish to the net. Instruct the kids who've tied their fish to the net to keep going back for more people to tie their fish to the net. (You may want to sing a favorite song while the group finishes tying all the fish to the net.)

Gather group members around the net and instruct them to hold it in their hands. Discuss what the net looks like now with all the fish tied to it. Ask kids to pray aloud if they wish; they don't need to add to the prayer in any specific order. Say that you'll conclude the prayer.

Display the net in the meeting room for the next few weeks. Use the fish as reminders of our call to be fishers of men and women. Follow up at future meetings by asking how the witnessing went. Challenge kids to invite and bring their "fish" to church and youth group meetings!

Family Feelings

. . . .

Purpose

To express feelings about family relationships

Materials

For each person:
- two sheets of construction paper or old news-papers
- pencil

Action

Form groups of no more than six. Give each person one sheet of paper. Say: Do something to this paper to indicate how you feel about your family right now. Maybe you'll tear it into a shape or fold it or crumple it.

Allow time for participants to act.

Reflection

In their groups, have kids each respond to this question:
- How did you feel when you were tearing, folding or crumpling your paper? (Some may say, "I felt angry as I tore it into little shreds" or "I felt in control of my family as I ripped each shape.")

Interpretation

In their groups, have kids each respond to this question:
- How is this paper like your family? (Some may say,

"This crumpled ball is like my family because we're close even though we argue sometimes" or "These three pieces are me, my sister and my mom. This piece far away is my dad because he doesn't live with us anymore.")

Application

Have a young person read aloud Colossians 3:12-14. Give kids each another sheet of paper and tell them to shape it into what they'd see as the perfect family. Have them each write on the new shape one action of love from the verses that they need to live out at home. For example: "I'll try to be more compassionate with my mom when she comes home from work. I'll help her when she's getting dinner ready and I'll set the table." Or "Since my dad left, I haven't been able to forgive him. I'll send him a letter about my feelings and say I forgive him." Have the kids each share with their group what they wrote.

Or Try This

This activity works especially well with kids experiencing family difficulty, such as divorce or other family conflicts. But you can also use this activity for other topics. Let kids explore their feelings toward school, youth group or church. It will spur them to action in those areas too.

How I Fit in My Family

. . . .

Purpose

To show how people relate to their family members

Materials

- none needed

Action

Form groups no larger than eight. Ask kids each to take turns creating a family sculpture by using the people in their group to represent their own family members. As the participants "sculpt" their families, have them each physically place the family members to symbolize where they fit in relationship to the other family members. For example, "Mom" and "Dad" placed apart could represent separation, or back to back with arms crossed could show lack of communication. Two "brothers" arm in arm near the parents could show the family's closeness. Each sculptor must be in the sculpture to represent himself or herself.

Lead the Reflection and Interpretation sections between turns so kids each can explain their sculpture.

Reflection

In their groups, have kids each respond to this question:

- How did you feel sculpting your family? (Some may say, "I never realized how much distance I feel from my mother. I wanted to put her in the other room." Or "I feel close to my brother and it felt good to put us close together.")

Interpretation

In their groups, have kids each respond to this question:

● How is this experience like or unlike your real family? (Some may say, "It's unlike my family because I have no control to get them to do anything I want. But I could move them around and control them in the sculpture." Or "This is just like my family because we're each in our own little corner of the world.")

Application

Have kids each tell one discovery they gained from this experience. Then have them each tell what they will do the next time they see each family member.

Read aloud Ephesians 3:14-19: "For this reason I kneel before the Father, from whom his whole family in heaven and on earth derives its name. I pray that out of his glorious riches he may strengthen you with power through his Spirit in your inner being, so that Christ may dwell in your hearts through faith. And I pray that you, being rooted and established in love, may have power, together with all the saints, to grasp how wide and long and high and deep is the love of Christ, and to know this love that surpasses knowledge— that you may be filled to the measure of all the fullness of God."

Conclude with a sculptor's prayer: Have each person take turns standing in the center of the group. The group offers a prayer for the person in the middle by "sculpting" that person into a "prayer offering." For example, the group might pray that Corey can be more open to his father and then sculpt Corey on his knees with arms open wide. Or they might pray that Bonnie can listen more intently to her sister and sculpt Bonnie leaning forward with her hands cupping her ears.

Or Try This

You can also use sculpting to have kids demonstrate how they feel about school, their friendships, their lives, their future—even the youth group. The possibilities are endless!

The One-Way to Two-Way

. . . .

Purpose

To witness the value of two-way communication

Materials

For every two people:
- blank sheet of paper
- simple line drawing that's different from any of the other pairs' (Simple geometric shapes and designs work well. If your group has more than 15 people, you can repeat some of the drawings.)

For each person:
- pencil
- paper
- envelope
- postage stamp

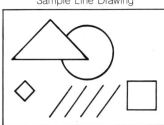

Sample Line Drawing

Action

Have each person link up with a partner. Have partners sit back to back. Then give these instructions: I'll hand out a drawing, face down, to one person in each pair. Make sure your partner doesn't see the drawing. Then I'll give a pencil and a blank sheet of paper to the other person in your twosome. The person with the drawing must describe the picture without saying what it is, so the partner can draw it. But the person drawing can't speak—or peek! And it won't help to look at other pairs' pictures because they're all different. Don't turn around and check your artistic work until I give the signal.

Allow a few minutes for drawing. Call time and let pairs chuckle and compare their drawings.

Reflection

In their pairs, have kids each respond to this question:

● How did you feel during this experience? (Some may say, "It was frustrating because I couldn't understand what my partner meant" or "I felt amazed that we got the drawings to match as well as they did!")

Interpretation

In their pairs, have kids each respond to these questions:

● How is this like real people-to-people communication? (Some may say, "It's terrible when only one person does all the talking" or "It's so much better if we could be face to face and ask questions.")

● Why is two-way communication so important? (Some may say, "It helps you understand each other better" or "Better things can be accomplished when both participate equally.")

● What happens when communication is only one-way? (Some may say, "People don't understand each other as well" or "There are lots more chances for misunderstandings.")

Application

Hand out paper and a pencil to each person. Tell young people to make a communication chart by drawing two columns on the paper and dividing each column into thirds, then numbering the column sections with #1, #2, #3. (See the example.)

Then say: In section one, column one, write the name of someone with whom you share great two-way communication and why.

In section two, column one, write the name of some-

Communication Chart

1	1
2	2
3	3

one with whom you don't communicate very well and why.

In section three, column one, write one way you communicate with God.

Have partners discuss their answers.

Invite a young person to read aloud Matthew 7:7-12.

Say: In section one, column two, write an action you'll take to thank the person you share great communication with. (For example, write a pocm or call.)

In section two, column two, write an action you'll take to improve communication with the person you're struggling with. (For example, stop butting in when that person talks, or repeat what I think I hear the other person saying.)

In section three, column two, write an action you'll take to improve your prayer life. (For example, spend five minutes each morning in prayer, or initiate meal prayers at home.)

Have partners tell each other what they've written. Then have each person self-address an envelope and seal his or her own paper inside it. Collect these envelopes.

Tell group members that you'll send these sheets to them in one month as a reminder to keep their commitments.

Or Try This

You can also use this technique with New Year's resolutions and return the envelopes to the kids one year later!

Burnout

Purpose

To explore feelings of stress and burnout

Materials

For every six people:
- one matchbook
- paper
- pencil

For the whole group:
- one freestanding candle
- prize for one group of six people (For instance, a bunch of bananas could represent "going bananas," or crazy, decorative Band-Aids could represent "healing burnout.")

Action

Form groups no larger than six. Give each group a book of matches and this explanation: Choose a scribe to record all your group's answers on paper. Each person will light a match and before the match burns out name as many things as possible that cause stress and burnout in his or her life. Once the match burns out, pass the matchbook to another person, who must light a match and add to the list without repeating any of the stresses mentioned earlier. When the matchbook gets to the scribc, hc or she must find a replacement scribe for that turn. Continue around the circle until I say stop. If you have more than one group, your group is competing against the others. Whoever has the longest list wins a grand prize!

After the matchbook has made it around at least once, call time.

Award the prize to the group with the longest list. (If you have only one group, give it the prize when you're finished playing.) Applaud and have a few laughs.

Reflection

In their groups, have kids each respond to these questions:

● How did you feel listing the causes of stress while the match was burning? (Some may say, "I felt under pressure" or "I was afraid I might get burned.")

● How did you feel competing with the other groups? (Some may say, "I wanted to win so that caused even more stress" or "I felt it was unfair because my match went out so soon.")

Interpretation

In their groups, have kids each respond to these questions:

● How are these feelings similar to your feelings when you're under pressure? (Some may say, "When I take a test in school, I get that same feeling of tension" or "Being on the basketball team puts me under stress because we want to beat all the other teams.")

● How do you cope with feelings of stress and pressure? (Some may say, "I try to laugh it off" or "I eat and listen to my stereo.")

● When is pressure good? (Some may say, "When it spurs you on to do a good job" or "When you want to do your part so the rest of the team benefits.")

● When is pressure dangerous? (Some may say, "When you get burned out because you don't know when to quit—like not blowing the match out before it got to your fingers" or "When you do things that harm your body or relationships.")

Application

Turn out all the lights. Have one person light a candle in the middle of the room. Have a young person read aloud John 14:27. Encourage each person to focus on the lighted candle in silence. Challenge participants to pray for the peace that Jesus Christ offers amid the stresses and pressures in their lives. Say you'll allow about five minutes for individual silent prayer.

After five minutes, read aloud Matthew 6:25-34: "Therefore I tell you, do not worry about your life, what you will eat or drink; or about your body, what you will wear. Is not life more important than food, and the body more important than clothes? Look at the birds of the air; they do not sow or reap or store away in barns, and yet your heavenly Father feeds them. Are you not much more valuable than they? Who of you by worrying can add a single hour to his life?

"And why do you worry about clothes? See how the lilies of the field grow. They do not labor or spin. Yet I tell you that not even Solomon in all his splendor was dressed like one of these. If that is how God clothes the grass of the field, which is here today and tomorrow is thrown into the fire, will he not much more clothe you, O you of little faith? So do not worry, saying, 'What shall we eat?' or 'What shall we drink?' or 'What shall we wear?' For the pagans run after all these things, and your heavenly Father knows that you need them. But seek first his kingdom and his righteousness, and all these things will be given to you as well. Therefore do not worry about tomorrow, for tomorrow will worry about itself. Each day has enough trouble of its own."

Conclude by saying: Go in peace.

Can You Serve Two Masters?

Purpose

To demonstrate how we try to block out Jesus

Materials

- stacks of newspapers
- garbage bags

Action

Form groups no larger than eight. Have one person in each group lie on the floor with arms outstretched like a cross. Tell the others to gather around that person. Have them wad up newspapers to pile on the person. Instruct them to cover the person so no one can see him or her.

Halt the activity when the bodies are sufficiently buried. Keep the people under the piles.

Reflection

In their groups, have the people under the papers each respond to these questions:

- How does it feel to be buried under the papers? (Some may say, "Help! I don't like it!" or "I feel really far away from everybody else.")

Tell the people to burst out from under the papers. Then ask:

- How does it feel to be free from all the clutter? (Some may say, "Whew! I can breathe again!" or "I'm glad to get out of there!")

Ask all the other people:

- How did you feel as you were covering up the person with newspapers? (Some may say, "I was having a blast!" or "I started worrying about the person underneath.")

Interpretation

In their groups, have kids each respond to these questions:

● How is that person like Jesus in our lives? (Some may say, "We get so busy with other stuff, he just disappears out of our lives" or "The way the person was lying reminded me of the cross; I felt like I was stoning or crucifying him.")

● What are the things in your life (like the newspapers) that stand in the way of your relationship with Jesus? (Some may say, "My friends make fun of me for going to church so I don't go" or "My job and wanting money keep me from spending time with other Christians and getting involved in Bible study.")

Invite a young person to read aloud Luke 16:13. Ask each person:

● How is this verse like the experience of burying the person? (Some may say, "You can't see Jesus when you get concerned about 'things' in your life" or "In the midst of having a crazy time we forget what's really important—Jesus.")

● Does this mean money and material possessions are bad or dangerous? Why or why not? (Some may say, "They're only bad when they 'cover up' spending time with God" or "They're dangerous if that's all you think about.")

Application

Use uncrumpled newspapers to make the shape of a cross.

Have people each tear a piece of newspaper into the shape of something in their life that stands in the way of their relationship with Jesus.

Without using words, have each person show the group the newspaper symbol, crumple it and offer it at the foot of the newspaper cross.

Close by reading Luke 16:13 one more time: "No servant can serve two masters. Either he will hate the one and love the other, or he will be devoted to the one and despise the other. You cannot serve both God and Money."

Have kids gather the newspapers into the garbage bags.

Alone

· ·

Purpose

To experience the pain of being all alone

Materials

● none needed

Action

Form a circle. (If your group is too large to make one circle in the room, form small circles of no more than six people.)

Say: Sometimes we think we don't need God or don't need to be around other Christians. We feel like we can make it on our own.

Have kids stand facing the center of the circle. Tell everybody to turn to the right. Now have them outstretch their arms like a cross, not touching anyone else. Have participants close their eyes while you read the psalmist's words.

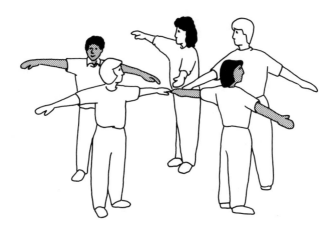

Read Psalm 69:1-16 slowly:

"Save me, O God,
for the waters have come up to my neck.
I sink in the miry depths, where there is no foothold.
I have come into the deep waters; the floods engulf me.
I am worn out calling for help; my throat is parched.
My eyes fail, looking for my God.
Those who hate me without reason outnumber the hairs of
    my head;
many are my enemies without cause, those who seek to
    destroy me.
I am forced to restore what I did not steal.
You know my folly, O God;
my guilt is not hidden from you.
May those who hope in you not be disgraced because of
    me,
O Lord, the Lord Almighty;
may those who seek you not be put to shame because of
    me, O God of Israel.
For I endure scorn for your sake, and shame covers my face.
I am a stranger to my brothers, an alien to my own mother's
    sons;
for zeal for your house consumes me, and the insults of
    those who insult you fall on me.
When I weep and fast, I must endure scorn;
when I put on sackcloth, people make sport of me.
Those who sit at the gate mock me, and I am the song of
    the drunkards."

Pause and say: Turn to your left and put your arms on
the shoulders of the two nearest people. Use the people
around you because they are the support God has placed in
your life.

Continue reading the Psalm:

"But I pray to you, O Lord, in the time of your favor;
in your great love, O God, answer me with your sure
    salvation.

Rescue me from the mire, do not let me sink;
deliver me from those who hate me, from the deep waters.
Do not let the floodwaters engulf me
or the depths swallow me up
or the pit close its mouth over me.
Answer me, O Lord, out of the goodness of your love;
in your great mercy turn to me."

Reflection

Form groups of no more than six people. In their groups, have kids each respond to these questions:

● How did you feel during the first part of the Psalm? (Some may say, "Horrible!" or "I felt like I was going to die!")

● How did you feel when you were able to rest your arms on others? (Some may say, "It felt so good" or "It felt like a great relief.")

Interpretation

In their groups, have kids each respond to these questions:

● How is this experience like the times we don't seek help? (Some may say, "In the end, going it alone causes a lot of pain" or "It's no fun being on your own.")

● How is this experience like the relief of reaching out to God and others for help? (Some may say, "It feels great, but we often don't reach out soon enough" or "It really feels good knowing someone cares and will support you.")

● How does God use prayer and other people as support? (Some may say, "When I can take my troubles to God in prayer it takes a load off me" or "God seems to provide just the people I need when I need a listening ear.")

● Compare your outstretched arms to Jesus on the cross. How does that make you feel? (Some may say, "I'm grateful that Jesus took the pain for me" or "I never knew how much that would hurt.")

Application

Have kids each tell about a time in their life when they wanted to do things on their own—without the help of friends, parents or God. Then have them each tell about a time when they reached out for help. Encourage them each to compare the two times and what made the two times different.

Close by getting back into the original circle with arms around each other's shoulders. Go around the circle with each person adding one word to a prayer. For example, the word could be "help," "thanks" or the name of a person who's been a support. Tell group members that if someone else uses their word, that's okay. For a new twist, tell kids to pray with their eyes open.

Who Are the Least of These, Anyway?

. . . .

Purpose

To grow more sensitive to others' needs

Materials

For each person:
- 3×5 card
- pencil

For the whole group:
- assorted props (hats, towels, water pitchers, strings, garbage bags)

Action

Distribute a 3×5 card and pencil to each person. Say: Jesus talked about reaching out to the "least of these." Most of the time we think it's pretty easy to picture the "least of these"—the poor, the hungry, the homeless, the prisoners. But sometimes we don't recognize "the least of these" because they're so close to us. On your 3×5 card, finish this sentence: "A time I feel like the 'least of these' is . . ." Maybe it's when you fail a test or get yelled at or when you feel like nobody wants to talk to you. Don't sign your name. When you're finished, pass it in.

(Plan for an adult to sort through the 3×5 cards and choose six, 12 or 18 cards, depending on whether your group is small, medium or large, respectively. The person should select the cards by eliminating duplicates and choosing universal or special hurts.)

Designate one person to portray Jesus, and divide the rest of the group into 12 teams (a team could be one person). If you have fewer than 13 kids, assign more than one part to each person. If your group is much larger, have one group portray food feeders and another group portray food hoarders. Likewise, have one group as the waterers and a separate group as water hoarders, and so on for all the rest of the characters.

Have each team decide on words and actions that portray one of the following characters:

- Jesus (one person)
- Hungry people
- Food feeders/food hoarders
- Thirsty people
- Waterers/water hoarders
- Strangers
- Welcomers/shunners
- Naked people
- Clothers/clothes hoarders
- Sick people
- Caretakers/non-caretakers
- Prisoners
- Visitors/imprisoners

After teams have decided on actions for each character, tell the young people they'll be portraying these characters as Matthew 25, the famous "unto the least of these" passage, is read.

Have fun! Spark teams' creativity with wild and wacky props. (We've used anything from tablecloths and towels to crepe paper streamers and cardboard barrels with suspenders!) Allow a few minutes for teams to scamper around for props and to practice.

Read aloud the following scripture (or let one of your kids read it), allowing time for teams to do their thing. You may need to cue them at times. But that will just add to the fun!

A Paraphrase of Matthew 25:31-46

When the Son of Man comes in his glory,

> (Pause for Jesus to make a grand entrance)

and all the angels with him, he will sit on his throne in heavenly glory.

> (Pause for Jesus to sit on his "royal" throne—or nearest folding chair)

All the nations will be gathered before him,

> (Lead the group in a rousing round of applause and cheers)

and he will separate the people one from another

> (Pause for Jesus to make sweeping motions with his arms)

as a shepherd separates the sheep from the goats. He will put the sheep on his right and the goats on his left. Then the King will say to those on his right, "Come, you who are blessed by my Father; take your inheritance, the kingdom prepared for you since the creation of the world. For I was hungry

> (Pause for hungry to do their part)

and you gave me something to eat,

> (Pause for food feeders to do their part)

I was thirsty

> (Pause for thirsty to do their part)

and you gave me something to drink,

> (Pause for waterers to do their part)

I was a stranger

> (Pause for strangers to do their part)

and you invited me in,

> (Pause for welcomers to do their part)

I needed clothes

> (Pause for naked to do their part)

and you clothed me,

> (Pause for clothers to do their part)

I was sick
(Pause for sick to do their part)
and you looked after me,
(Pause for caretakers to do their part)
I was in prison
(Pause for prisoners to do their part)
and you came to visit me.''
(Pause for visitors to do their part)
Then the righteous will answer him, ''Lord,
when did we see you hungry
(Pause for hungry to do their part)
and feed you,
(Pause for food feeders to do their part)
or thirsty
(Pause for thirsty to do their part)
and give you something to drink?
(Pause for waterers to do their part)
When did we see you a stranger
(Pause for strangers to do their part)
and invite you in,
(Pause for welcomers to do their part)
or needing clothes
(Pause for naked to do their part)
and clothe you?
(Pause for clothers to do their part)
When did we see you sick
(Pause for sick to do their part)
and take care of you,
(Pause for caretakers to do their part)
or in prison
(Pause for prisoners to do their part)
and go to visit you?''
(Pause for visitors to do their part)
The King will reply, ''I tell you the truth, what-
ever you did for one of the least of these
brothers of mine, you did for me.''
Then he will say to those on his left, ''Depart
from me, you who are cursed,

(Pause for Jesus to make "banishing" motions)
into the eternal fire prepared for the devil and his angels.
For I was hungry
(Pause for hungry to do their part)
and you gave me nothing to eat,
(Pause for food hoarders to do their part)
I was thirsty
(Pause for thirsty to do their part)
and you gave me nothing to drink,
(Pause for water hoarders to do their part)
I was a stranger
(Pause for strangers to do their part)
and you did not invite me in,
(Pause for shunners to do their part)
I needed clothes
(Pause for the naked to do their part)
and you did not clothe me,
(Pause for clothes hoarders to do their part)
I was sick,
(Pause for sick to do their part)
and you did not look after me.
(Pause for non-caretakers to do their part)
I was in prison
(Pause for prisoners to do their part)
and you did not come to visit me."
(Pause for imprisoners to do their part)
They also will answer, "Lord, when did we see you hungry
(Pause for hungry to do their part)
or thirsty
(Pause for thirsty to do their part)
or a stranger
(Pause for strangers to do their part)
or needing clothes
(Pause for the naked to do their part)
or sick
(Pause for sick to do their part)

or in prison,
(Pause for prisoners to do their part)
and did not help you?"
He will reply,
(Pause for Jesus to stand and gesture)
"I tell you the truth, whatever you did not do for
one of the least of these, you did not do for me."
Then they will go away to eternal punishment,
but the righteous to eternal life.

Applaud the group's efforts.

Reflection

Have people stay in their acting teams. In their groups, have kids each respond to this question:

● How did you feel playing the part you played? (Some may say, "I felt awkward, like I couldn't relate" or "I felt a little hurt when the people refused to help me.")

Interpretation

In their teams, have kids each respond to these questions:

● How are you like any of the characters portrayed? Why? (Some may say, "I'm most like the people who reached out in love, because I like to be giving" or "I felt most like the ones who refused to welcome the strangers because I feel uncomfortable making new friends.")

● Are you most often like the needy, the givers or the ones who refused to help? Explain. (Some may say, "Lately I've been feeling like the needy because things in my life haven't been going so good." Or "I hate to admit it, but I'm most like the ones who didn't reach out. I get too caught up in my own life to think about anybody else.")

Application

In their teams, have kids each respond to these questions:

● Who are two "least of these" people in your life

right now? What could you do to reach out to them? (Some may say, "My mom and dad seem to be like the 'least of these' because they seem emotionally and spiritually needy. I could cooperate with them more and not give them so much trouble by arguing all the time." Or "I know a family that doesn't have any money for new clothes because nobody has a job. If I could get up my courage I could give some of the clothes I have to help them out.")

Remind kids that needy people are all around them. With a volunteer's help, pray the following prayer, lifting up the concerns and needs written earlier on the 3×5 cards by the group members.

"The Least of These" Prayer

I was hungry.

(Have volunteer read one to three responses from the 3×5 cards written earlier.)

I was thirsty.

(Have volunteer read one to three responses from the 3×5 cards written earlier.)

I was a stranger.

(Have volunteer read one to three responses from the 3×5 cards written earlier.)

I was naked.

(Have volunteer read one to three responses from the 3×5 cards written earlier.)

I was sick.

(Have volunteer read one to three responses from the 3×5 cards written earlier.)

I was in prison.

(Have volunteer read one to three responses from the 3×5 cards written earlier.)

Lord, open our eyes to the least of these, those standing right beside us. Give us courage and strength to reach out in love. In your name we pray, amen.

"Bill"

Purpose
To reach out to someone fragile and in need

Materials
- large weather balloons (at least two, in case one breaks when blowing it up)

Get weather balloons at a local army surplus store or order from Group Publishing, Box 481, Loveland, CO 80539. Group offers 8-foot balloons for $12.95 each.

- a hair blow-dryer with a "cool" setting (for blowing up the weather balloon)
- masking tape (for closing off the balloon's opening)

Action
Prior to kids' arrival, use a blow-dryer to inflate an 8-foot balloon to about 4 or 5 feet in diameter. Place the balloon near where you'll be speaking. The huge balloon will build your young people's curiosity and anticipation. Ask them not to touch it.

Tell "Bill's Story."

Slowly, gently pass "Bill" (the blown-up weather balloon) into the group. Be very careful because weather balloons pop easily.

Observe how the group responds. After a few minutes, bring the balloon forward and talk about what happened. If Bill pops, move right to the Reflection section.

Bill's Story

I've brought someone with me today. I want you to meet him. His name is Bill. He goes to my school. And I think he goes to your school. I think you know Bill.

He's not the best-looking guy in school. He's a little overweight—no, he's a lot overweight. His clothes aren't the best. He has lots of pimples. It seems like his hair is always messed up. Some of us have wondered if he ever takes a shower.

You know Bill. He's the one who, when he walks down the hall, half the kids walk way over on the other side of the hall—just to avoid getting close to him.

You know Bill. He's the one who eats his lunch alone—every day. You've seen him sitting at the end table in the cafeteria. All alone. Nobody wants to sit next to Bill. Oh, once I thought about doing my Christian duty by sitting next to him. But then I thought, I've got a reputation to uphold. I can't be seen with . . . Bill!

But, you know something? Lately I've gotten to know Bill. And I've found out he's just like you and me. He's fragile, just like you and me. You remember all those unkind things we've said about Bill? You know how those little putdowns don't seem to faze him? Well, I found out that every unkind word cuts him like a knife—just like it would you or me. He's fragile. And I've also learned that when somebody says one kind word to him or even just gives him a smile, he soars! He could go a whole week on one nice word. He's fragile and sensitive.

I've brought Bill with me because I know you. I believe you'll be able to touch Bill in a special way today. In a moment I'll introduce Bill, and I'd like each of you to have a chance to reach out to Bill with the

hand of Christian love. But I must warn you—he's
very fragile. Something could easily happen in this
room that would cause Bill to break. If we get rough
with Bill—even if we think we're doing it in fun—he'll
break. But if we work together with kindness, all of
us will have a chance to touch Bill. Now I'd like you
to meet Bill.

Reflection

Form groups no larger than six. In their groups, have
kids each respond to these questions:
● How did you feel during the experience? (Some may
say, "I felt good because everyone was so careful and car-
ing" or "I was angry when some of the people started
clowning around and got careless, and Bill broke.")
● How did you feel when you got to touch Bill? (Some
may say, "I wanted to be very gentle and kind" or "I was so
glad I got to touch him because for a while I thought I
might not get to.")
● How did you feel if you didn't get to touch Bill?
(Some may say, "I felt sad" or "I didn't want to touch Bill
because I didn't want the responsibility if he broke.")
● How did you feel when Bill popped (or he didn't
pop)? (Some may say, "I felt so bad, like I'd done something
to hurt him" or "I felt almost like somebody had just died.")

Interpretation

In their groups, have kids each respond to these questions:
● How is Bill like the kids at school? at youth group?
(Some may say, "At first we were gentle, but then we got
rougher and it became a funny game—then Bill broke, just
like the kids at school who can't take it anymore. Even if
our jokes are just in fun it hurts." Or "I didn't want to
touch him; I wanted to get rid of him and that's what we

do with 'undesirable' people around us.")

● Have you ever felt like Bill? Tell about it.

● How do people's reactions help or hurt the "Bills" in our lives? (Some may say, "When we reach out in love, we can make all the difference in the world" or "Our thoughtlessness can be more damaging than we ever know.")

Application

Read aloud Philippians 2:3-5: "Do nothing out of selfish ambition or vain conceit, but in humility consider others better than yourselves. Each of you should look not only to your own interests, but also to the interests of others. Your attitude should be the same as that of Christ Jesus."

Have each person think of a "Bill" in his or her own life. Say: Tell your group about that person. Then say how you will reach out in Christian love to that person and when you will do it.

Encourage each small group to close in prayer.

You Are the Light of the World

Purpose

To give and receive affirmation

Materials

For every six to eight people:

- one candle with a drip-guard and matches, or a Cyalume stick (You can purchase Cyalume sticks from Group Publishing, Box 481, Loveland, CO 80539 for $1.60 each.)

Action

Form a circle with no more than eight people. Hand a lighted candle (or Cyalume stick) to each group. Say: Begin with the person holding the light. That person will say something he or she appreciates about someone in the circle—without saying that person's name. For example, "I really appreciate this person because whenever I feel down I can count on this person to lift my spirits." Without saying the recipient's name, the person with the light hands the light to the person just described. Then the person receiving the light does the same for someone else in the group.

Continue by saying: There are only three guidelines: (1) You must say something positive. This isn't the time to clown around. (2) You must make sure each person receives the light at least once. (3) You may receive the light more than once.

Dim the room lights. Allow 10 to 15 minutes for the experience. When you feel it's appropriate, signal that the person holding the light will be the last to speak.

Reflection

In their groups, have kids each respond to this question:

● How did you feel during this experience? (Some may say, "I felt really warm and good inside" or "I felt a sense of anticipation wondering who the person was talking about.")

Interpretation

In their groups, have kids each respond to these questions:

● How is this experience like giving and receiving compliments in real life? (Some may say, "It feels good to give compliments because it brightens someone's day" or "In real life I feel uncomfortable receiving praise.")

● How did you feel giving compliments? (Some may say, "I loved making other people feel good by telling them what I like about them" or "I liked giving affirmation—especially when the person didn't expect it.")

● How did you feel receiving compliments? (Some may say, "I loved it!" or "I got so embarrassed.")

● Which was more difficult for you—to give or receive? Why? (Some may say, "Giving was hardest because I have a hard time being serious about stuff like this" or "I felt so self-conscious when I got a compliment that I always wanted to say, 'No, that's not true' or 'You don't mean that.' ")

● How is giving and receiving praise like bringing Christ's light to someone's life? (Some may say, "Telling people they mean something to you makes them feel worthwhile and special. That's what Jesus' love does." Or "Graciously receiving a compliment helps the giver know you value that person's views. It conveys God's unconditional acceptance.")

Application

Have a young person read aloud Matthew 5:14-16. Encourage group members each to choose someone who isn't present and tell how they will light up that person's life this week. For example, someone might choose to surprise a parent with a note that says, "I love you and God loves you." Or someone could select a loner classmate to have lunch with and get to know better.

Unless You Become Like a Child

Purpose

To understand what Jesus means by "childlike faith"

Materials

For each person:
- a wooden or cardboard toy block

Action

Surprise the group by announcing: Let's play Ring Around the Rosie!

Form small groups no larger than eight. Listen and watch for people's reactions (groans, embarrassment, skepticism). Play a few times. If time permits, play other childhood favorites such as London Bridge or Drop the Hankie.

Reflection

In their groups, have kids each respond to these questions:

- How did you feel when you heard the announcement to play Ring Around the Rosie? (Some may say, "I felt silly and stupid" or "I felt like it was going to be fun and crazy.")

- What were your feelings during the game? (Some may say, "I was embarrassed and hoped no one would walk by and see us" or "I felt free and uninhibited.")

Interpretation

In their groups, have kids each respond to these questions:

● How are those feelings like or unlike the feelings we have about accepting Jesus or sharing our Christian faith? (Some may say, "I'm so afraid of what other people will think that I don't feel comfortable witnessing about my faith" or "Sometimes I think people think Christians are weird or stupid for believing in Jesus.")

Now give each person a toy block. Have small group members build a wall with their blocks by each stacking a block as they tell what creates barriers to accepting Jesus with a childlike faith and sharing him with others. For example, fear of what others might think or the inability to trust.

Application

Read aloud Matthew 18:1-5: "At that time the disciples came to Jesus and asked, 'Who is the greatest in the kingdom of heaven?' He called a little child and had him stand among them. And he said: 'I tell you the truth, unless you change and become like little children, you will never enter the kingdom of heaven. Therefore, whoever humbles himself like this child is the greatest in the kingdom of heaven. And whoever welcomes a little child like this in my name welcomes me.' "

Have kids each think of a positive childlike quality they need to put into action in their own lives, such as trust, forgiveness, openness. Before they begin sharing, have groups each decide what faith symbol they'd like to build with their blocks. Spark their creativity by suggesting they turn their wall into a cross or fish. As kids each tell their group the positive childlike quality, have them pick up their block and use it to build the faith symbol.

Conclude with the entire group singing "Jesus Loves Me."

The Carwash Blues

. . . .

Purpose

To explore fairness and God's grace

Materials

● none needed

Action

Form five groups (a group could be one person). Explain that you're going to experience a fun, paraphrased version of Matthew 20:1-15 (the workers in the vineyard). Assign each group one of the five identities, sounds and actions from the chart on page 130.

Once you've assigned the parts and had groups practice, read the following story—having each group respond on cue. For fun, replace the name "Pam" with your own adult senior high worker's name.

Matthew 20:1-15

(a paraphrase)

Plans were made for the annual "clean-your-car day" at church. The event was sponsored by the youth group, who planned to raise money for an upcoming summer trip. Pam, the senior high worker, had gotten out the publicity and made sure someone gathered all the buckets, brushes, sponges, hoses and soap. She promised each person who worked at the carwash $25 worth of credit for the trip.

The April day came, clear and warm, perfect for washing cars—and a welcome change after the dreary winter rains. When the **Early Birds** arrived, cars were already in line and waiting. The **Early Birds** dove into their task with vigor, but the line continued to grow. Still, the **Early Birds** worked. Pam worried that she might have done too well on the publicity.

At 8:30 a.m. she called more young people. Since it was still early in the day, she promised them the full $25 too. They agreed to be there at 9 a.m. Sure enough, the **Nine-to-fives** showed up right on time. The **Early Birds** were glad. The **Nine-to-fives** were a big help.

But the line of muddy cars continued to stretch. No matter how fast the sponges moved and the soap-suds flew, the **Early Birds** and the **Nine-to-fives** just couldn't keep up. Pam knew what she had to do. She went into the church and called the kids who had stayed out late for last night's high school dance. After they were told the problem and promised $25 worth of credit, the **Sleep-til-nooners** came and started work right beside the **Nine-to-fives**. The **Early Birds** were glad to see the **Sleep-til-nooners** arrive.

The **Sleep-til-nooners** made a contribution, but it wasn't much. Cars lined up across the church parking lot and out into the street. By now the **Nine-to-fives** had shriveled fingers. Pam needed reinforcements. She searched the group list and called a few of the people who were supposed to be there but hadn't shown up. "Why aren't you helping?" she inquired. "Nobody asked us," they said, "but we are free after 3 p.m. and would like to go on the trip. The $25 sure would help." So the **Free-after-threes** came to the church and worked.

Well, folks, the **Early Birds**, the **Nine-to-fives**, the **Sleep-til-nooners**, and the **Free-after-threes** washed more cars than they could count. You might say the carwash was a splash hit. Dirty, dusty vehicles were transformed. Still they came. Pam was worried about whether they could wash all the cars.

Finally, she called everyone else on the youth group list and promised to give each a $25 credit for helping. This last group, the **Happy-hour-chargers**, worked with the **Nine-to-fives**; the **Free-after-threes** worked with the **Early Birds**; and the **Sleep-til-nooners** worked with everyone.

With the **Happy-hour-chargers'** help, the last car was finally washed. As it sparkled out of sight, Pam called the group together. She got out her book, and as kids stood around her, she gave them their due. Pam gave $25 worth of credit each to the **Early Birds**, $25 each to the **Nine-to-fives**, $25 each to the **Sleep-til-nooners**, $25 each to the **Free-after-threes**, and $25 each to the **Happy-hour-chargers**.

With their receipts in hand, the **Early Birds** began to grumble: "We don't mean to be in a fowl mood, but we **Early Birds** worked a lot harder and longer than these **Nine-to-fives**, these lazy **Sleep-til-nooners**, these free-loading **Free-after-threes** and certainly these hopeless **Happy-hour-chargers**. Why, they hardly washed a windshield! Where were the **Free-after-threes** when that big truck came through this morning? Pam, you sure don't know much about business!"

"Listen, folks," Pam answered. "I promised $25 worth of credit each to the **Happy-hour-chargers**, $25 each to the **Free-after-threes**, $25 each to the **Sleep-til-nooners**, $25 each to the **Nine-to-fives**, and I promised $25 each to the **Early Birds**. I haven't cheated you. We made an agreement. I want to give everyone this much. Are you jealous because I'm generous?"

So they all went home with their $25 credit for the trip in their hands.

Carwash Characters

Identity	Sound	Action
1. Early Birds (They get up early in the morning and work hard all day.)	Crow like roosters.	Flap arms.
2. Nine-to-fives (They work strictly from 9 a.m. to 5 p.m.)	Sing the first line "Working 9 to 5."	Look at watch.
3. Sleep-til-nooners (They take the morning easy and report to work at noon.)	Snore.	Lean head on shoulder.
4. Free-after-threes (They work only part time, starting at 3 p.m.)	Ask in unison, "There's a car-wash today?"	Shrug shoulders.
5. Happy-hour-chargers (They work only one hour, from 5 to 6 p.m.)	Make the bugle call to charge.	Hold up hands as if playing a bugle.

Reflection

Form groups of five having each group contain one person each from the *Early Birds, Nine-to-fives, Sleep-til-nooners, Free-after-threes,* and *Happy-hour-chargers.*

In their groups, have kids each respond to this question:

● How did you feel being the worker you were and getting the amount of money you did? How did you feel toward the other workers? (Some may say, "As an early-bird worker, I felt cheated because nobody else had to work as long" or "I felt guilty having come on board late in the day.")

Interpretation

In their groups, have kids each respond to these questions:

● When was a time you felt unappreciated or treated unfairly or got something you felt you really didn't deserve? Describe that time. (Some may say, "Last week after youth group, I didn't think it was fair that I got stuck cleaning up after everybody else left" or "My parents always yell at me when they get upset with my older brother, even though I haven't done anything wrong.")

● What do you think this parable teaches us about God's love? (Some may say, "God is generous and loves us no matter what." Or "God doesn't care if you've been a hard-working, faithful Christian all your life or if you're a brand new Christian. We're seen equally in God's eyes.")

● How does that perspective on God's love affect how we interact with each other? (Some may say, "We shouldn't think of ourselves as better than others" or "We need to realize we're all part of God's family—no matter what our age or background.")

Application

Have kids each think of one person they compare themselves with unfairly, such as a sister or brother or friend.

In their groups, have kids each respond to this question:

● How could looking at that person through God's eyes change your thoughts? (Some may say, "God loves that person, so I'll try to too" or "God doesn't care that I'm not as talented or good-looking as my friend; he still loves me.")

Close by having a young person read aloud 1 Corinthians 13.

Or Try This

This parable also works great if your group actually does carwashes or fund-raisers. This may hit close to your young people's actual experience and feelings of unfairness in the group. Use it to open discussion about who deserves to reap the benefits of the funds if someone hasn't worked as hard as everyone else.

The Matthew 20:1-15 paraphrase in the Action section is reprinted from *The Giving Book* by Paul M. Thompson and Joani Schultz. Copyright John Knox Press 1985. Used by permission of Westminister/John Knox Press.

A Parable of Talents

Purpose

To learn to appreciate and use God-given talents

Materials

For each person:
- paper
- pencil

Action

Have group members stand and face you. Explain that the group will experience an echo pantomime. Say: Simply say and do whatever I say and do.

Have fun! And be ready for some laughs!

A Parable of Talents

Words	Actions
A man was going on a trip.	*Heave a pretend garment bag over shoulder*
So he called his servants	*Wave hand to beckon*
And put them in charge.	*Salute*
He gave one 5,000 coins.	*Show five fingers, palm out*
Ooooh!	*Twist hand from palm to back, palm to back*
He gave one 2,000 coins	*Show two fingers, palm out*

Words	Action
Ahhhh!	*Twist hand with two fingers, from palm to back, palm to back*
And he gave one 1,000 coins.	*Show one finger, palm out*
Oh!	*Point one finger to brain*
Then the man left on his trip.	*Wave goodbye and turn completely around*
The servant with 5,000 coins	*Show five fingers, palm out*
(Pant, pant, pant)	*(Continue above motion)*
Invested 1-2-3-4-5.	*Point to each finger as you count*
The one with 2,000 coins	*Show two fingers, palm out*
Rushed to the bank.	*Run in place. Show two fingers, palm out, with other arm going back and forth (as in running)*
Whew!	*Wipe brow with free hand*
And invested too! 1-2!	*Point to each finger as you count*
But the other guy	*Hold up one finger and shake head "no"*
Dug a hole (Ugghh!)	*Pretend to shovel—Groan*
And hid his master's money.	*Touch the ground with one finger*
Oh-oh.	*Stand and hold up clenched fist*
After a long time	*Make sweeping motion with arm*
The master returned.	*Walk in place, pretending to carry a garment bag over shoulder*

Words	Actions
"Hi, everybody!	*Wave and smile*
Let's settle those accounts."	*Hands on hips*
So the one with 5,000 coins	*Show five fingers, palm out*
Handed over another five!	*Show five fingers, palms out for both hands*
Ooooh!	*Twist both hands from palm to back, palm to back*
"Well done!	*Applaud five times*
You good and faithful servant!	*Pat on back*
You've been faithful in managing small amounts,	*Show five fingers, palm out*
So I'll put you in charge of large amounts!	*Show both hands and flash 10 fingers open and closed*
Come, share my happiness!"	*Outstretch arms*
Then the one with 2,000 coins	*Show two fingers, palm out*
Said, "Here's another two!"	*Show each hand with two fingers*
Ahhhh!	*Twist both hands from palm to back, palm to back, showing two fingers on each hand*
"Well done!	*Applaud two times*
You good and faithful servant!	*Pat on back*
You've been faithful in managing small amounts,	*Show two fingers, palm out*

Words	Actions
So I'll put you in charge of large amounts!	*Show both hands and flash two fingers open and closed on each hand*
Come, share my happiness!"	*Outstretch arms*
Then came the servant with 1,000 coins.	*Point one finger up*
Oh-oh.	*Shake finger back and forth*
"I was afraid,	*Bite nails on one hand*
So afraid,	*Cover head with other hand and crouch in fear*
That I went off,	*Walk in place with head still covered, biting nails*
Dug a hole (Ugghh!)	*Pretend to shovel—Groan*
And hid your money.	*Wipe off dirt from hands*
Here's what belongs to you."	*Point one finger forward*
"You bad and lazy servant.	*Point same finger and shake it in admonition*
You didn't even invest it!"	*Throw hands up in air in disgust*
Here's the lesson to be learned:	*Place both arms at side*
To whom much is given,	*Raise left hand high*
Much is required.	*With left hand still raised, raise right hand*

Reflection

Form groups no larger than six. In their groups, have kids each respond to this question:

● How did you feel during the experience? (Some may say, "I felt a bit embarrassed" or "I felt playful and free.")

Interpretation

Say: This parable talks about "talents" in terms of money. But we can apply the same principles to anything God has given us, including our gifts and abilities.

In their groups, have kids respond to these questions:

● How are your feelings about the experience like or unlike the way you feel about your own gifts, abilities and talents? (Some may say, "Sometimes I feel embarrassed or afraid to use them" or "I'm thankful for what God has given me, and I enjoy doing what I can.")

● What message does this parable give you? (Some may say, "Don't hold back, give it all you've got" or "God expects you to use the gifts he has given you.")

● What does God want us to do with our gifts, abilities and talents? (Some may say, "He wants us to spread them around" or "He doesn't want us to be afraid and hold back from giving to others.")

● What do the amounts of talents given indicate? (Some may say, "Not everybody gets the same abilities" or "If you're gifted in anything, you're expected to use your gift—not bury it.")

Application

Hand out paper and pencils. Have young people each write five talents, abilities or gifts God has given them. Suggest not only musical or athletic abilities, but the more forgotten talents: organization, listening, kindness.

Then have each person choose one of their gifts and write a specific goal to use that gift to the fullest. Make sure the goal is specific, is measurable and has a start date. For example, one may write, "I like to talk with old people. By the end of the month I plan to visit an elderly shut-in."

Form trios to discuss the lists. Have kids tell about their goals within their trios, then exchange lists. Ask your young people to commit to pray for each other concerning the use of their talents.

Conclude by giving everyone a round of applause.

Standing Ovations

Purpose

To give and receive personal affirmation

Materials

- optional: the Olympic theme song and equipment to play it

Action

Form groups no larger than eight. Have each group determine whose birthday is closest to today. That person stands while the rest of the group remains seated on the floor. If you have chairs, have the person stand on a chair. Say: We're going to give the person standing a rousing, wild cheer and applause. I'll shout "Switch!" every little bit. That means another person must stand and receive the ovation.

Shout "Go!" and get ready for lots of noise! For an added celebration, play the Olympic fanfare.

After everyone has received an ovation, call time.

Reflection

In their groups, have kids each respond to these questions:

- How did you feel receiving the applause? (Some may say, "I loved it!" or "I felt self-conscious.")
- How did you feel giving the applause? (Some may say, "I felt good because it made someone else feel good" or "I was surprised how much fun clapping for someone could be.")

Interpretation

In their groups, have kids each respond to these questions:

● How is this experience like God's love? (Some may say, "We all got an ovation—like God's love is available to everyone" or "We didn't do anything to deserve it and that's like God's love.")

Read aloud Ephesians 2:8-10: "For it is by grace you have been saved, through faith—and this not from yourselves, it is the gift of God—not by works, so that no one can boast. For we are God's workmanship, created in Christ Jesus to do good works, which God prepared in advance for us to do."

● What does it mean that you're "saved by grace"? (Some may say, "It means you don't deserve it" or "It's a free gift.")

● How would you compare this verse to the experience you had with the ovation? (Some may say, "We didn't do anything to deserve it" or "It felt really good.")

Application

Allow time for silent prayer and meditation. Encourage kids each to reflect on God's unconditional love for them. Use this as a time for a new commitment to Jesus or a renewal of that relationship.

Close with a prayer of commitment and for awareness of God's unconditional love.

Be available to pray and talk with kids afterward.

Practical Resources for Your Youth Ministry

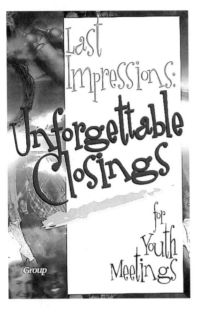

Last Impressions: Unforgettable Closings for Youth Meetings

Here's a collection of over 170 of Group's best-ever low-prep (or no-prep!) meeting closings...and each is tied to a thought-provoking Bible passage! With **Last Impressions** you'll be ready with thoughtful... affirming...issue-oriented...high-energy...prayerful...and servanthood closings—on a moment's notice!
1-55945-629-9

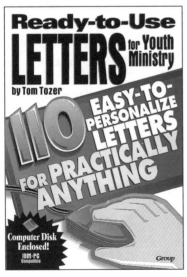

Ready-to-Use Letters for Youth Ministry
110 Easy-to-Personalize Letters for Practically Anything
Tom Tozer
These 110 already-written letters cover practically any situation that arises in youth ministry. And the included IBM-compatible computer disk makes adapting these letters quick and easy. You'll save hours of administrative time with this handy resource!
1-55945-692-2

More Practical Resources For Your Youth Ministry

Get Real: Making Core Christian Beliefs Relevant to Teenagers

Mike Nappa, Amy Nappa & Michael D.Warden

Here are the 24 Bible truths that Christian teenagers *must* know to survive in an unbelieving world. Included: proven strategies for effectively communicating these core Christian beliefs into the chaotic, fast-paced youth culture.
1-55945-708-2

Growing Close
Activities for Building Friendships and Unity in Youth Groups

These 150 practical, quick ideas help break the ice when teenagers don't know each other and break down cliques that often form in groups. A must-have resource for youth workers, coaches, camp directors, and Christian school teachers.
1-55945-709-0

For All Christian Educators...

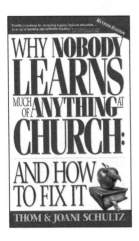

Why Nobody Learns Much Of Anything At Church: And How To Fix It
Thom & Joani Schultz

This book calls for sweeping change in Christian education...shows why it's needed...and how to do it. Anyone who teaches children, youth, or adults about the Christian faith will find practical, step-by-step solutions for *improving* how they provide Christian education. And this newly formatted, mass-market version is so inexpensive, everyone can afford a copy.
1-55945-902-6

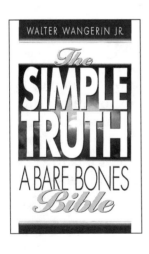

The Simple Truth: A Bare Bones Bible
Walter Wangerin Jr.

American Book Award winner Walter Wangerin Jr. shares major Bible stories in a simple but touching way. Readers new to the Bible will get a tantalizing taste of God's Word, and veteran Bible students will experience familiar stories in new, insightful ways.

hardcover   1-55945-630-2
softcover   1-55945-631-0

Capture Your Teenagers' Attention With Boredom-Busting, Topical, 4-week Studies for Junior and Senior High Students

FOR JUNIOR HIGH/MIDDLE SCHOOL:

Accepting Others: Beyond Barriers & Stereotypes	1-55945-126-2
Advice to Young Christians: Exploring Paul's Letters	1-55945-146-7
Applying the Bible to Life	1-55945-116-5
Becoming Responsible	1-55945-109-2
Bible Heroes: Joseph, Esther, Mary & Peter	1-55945-137-8
Boosting Self-Esteem	1-55945-100-9
Building Better Friendships	1-55945-138-6
Can Christians Have Fun?	1-55945-134-3
Christmas: A Fresh Look	1-55945-124-6
Doing Your Best	1-55945-142-4
Guys & Girls: Understanding Each Other	1-55945-110-6
Handling Conflict	1-55945-125-4
Heaven & Hell	1-55945-131-9
Is God Unfair?	1-55945-108-4
Making Parents Proud	1-55945-107-6
The Miracle of Easter	1-55945-143-2
Miracles!	1-55945-117-3
Peer Pressure	1-55945-103-3
Prayer	1-55945-104-1
Sermon on the Mount	1-55945-129-7
Telling Your Friends About Christ	1-55945-114-9
The Ten Commandments	1-55945-127-0
Today's Media: Choosing Wisely	1-55945-144-0
Today's Music: Good or Bad?	1-55945-101-7
What Is God's Purpose for Me?	1-55945-132-7
What's a Christian?	1-55945-105-X

FOR SENIOR HIGH:

Angels, Demons, Miracles & Prayer	1-55945-235-8
Christians in a Non-Christian World	1-55945-224-2
Communicating With Friends	1-55945-228-5
Dating Decisions	1-55945-215-3
Dealing With Life's Pressures	1-55945-232-3
Exploring Ethical Issues	1-55945-225-0
Faith for Tough Times	1-55945-216-1
Getting Along With Parents	1-55945-202-1
Getting Along With Your Family	1-55945-233-1
The Gospel of John: Jesus' Teachings	1-55945-208-0
Hazardous to Your Health: AIDS, Steroids & Eating Disorders	1-55945-200-5
Is Marriage in Your Future?	1-55945-203-X
The Joy of Serving	1-55945-210-2
Knowing God's Will	1-55945-205-6
Making Good Decisions	1-55945-209-9
Movies, Music, TV & Me	1-55945-213-7
Psalms	1-55945-234-X
Real People, Real Faith	1-55945-238-2
Revelation	1-55945-229-3
School Struggles	1-55945-201-3
Sex: A Christian Perspective	1-55945-206-4
Who Is God?	1-55945-218-8
Who Is Jesus?	1-55945-219-6
Who Is the Holy Spirit?	1-55945-217-X
Your Life as a Disciple	1-55945-204-8

Order today from your local Christian bookstore, or write: Group Publishing, P.O. Box 485, Loveland, CO 80539.

Index of Topics

Use this index to help you find experiences on a particular topic. The index lists themes that are covered in Chapter 7, as well as possible themes that you can bring out by modifying present activities.